THE
BASICS
OF. . .
Aeromodelling

Vic Smeed

NEXUS SPECIAL INTERESTS

Nexus Special Interests Ltd
Nexus House
Boundary Way
Hemel Hempstead
Herts HP2 7ST
England

First published 1995
© Vic Smeed 1995

ISBN 1-85486-113-1

Design and typesetting by The Studio, Exeter
Printed and bound in Great Britain by Bell & Bain Ltd., Glasgow

Contents

Introduction

Nowadays most of the general public seem to think that if it's a model aeroplane it must be radio controlled, forgetting (or not realising) that models were flying for almost a century before off-the-shelf radio equipment became available. You could actually buy ready-to-fly rubber models in the 1880s! Hundreds of modellers still prefer free-flight models — gliders, rubber or engine-powered designs — or control-line models to flying with radio, and, interestingly, their numbers are continually growing. However, it is some years since a book was available setting out the groundwork of successful model building and flying in relatively simple terms — a gap which it is hoped this book will go some way to fill.

Building models to fly need not be enormously expensive — a lot of enjoyment, not to mention knowledge, can be obtained with a couple of sheets of ordinary copy or typing paper and a length of kebab skewer. At a recent talk to a Cub Scouts troop, every lad made a paper glider. They all flew, and a simple distance competition created a great deal of fun and excitement, each boy standing in turn on a sturdy table to launch his model. From paper to simple balsa chuck gliders is not a big step, but one that can lead on to a lifelong hobby or even wider horizons. The number of people in the aerospace industry, many in high positions, who started from an interest in building models is really quite remarkable. On the other hand, there are many who become interested but do not progress because of disappointment at not being able to build or fly their first attempt; this is usually due to the fact that a totally unsuitable kitted model was purchased. There are excellent kits for beginners, or plans from which it is simple to build, and there is certainly no loss of face incurred by taking what is, after all, the commonsense approach.

Aeromodelling is now such a vast, many-faceted pursuit that it is virtually impossible to cover every aspect in detail in one book. This one seeks to set newcomers off on the right foot, whichever type of model they will ultimately favour. If it succeeds, well — see you on the flying field!

CHAPTER ONE

About models

Model flying pre-dated full-size aeroplanes by a century. There are vague references to 'artificial doves' and similar in early manuscripts and, of course, the da Vinci sketches of possible aircraft are well known, but the earliest evidence of fixed-wing flight (as opposed to balloons) refers to Sir George Cayley's experiments around 1800. Models played a large part in the development of flight and still contribute to research and testing; model flying for pleasure dates back to the rubber-powered Penaud models sold ready-to-fly in quite considerable quantities in the Paris area in the 1880s, but the real popularity of model building and flying only began in the 1930s, following the introduction of balsa coincident with a wave of airmindedness which swept the world.

Organised competitions date from around 1905–6, the models being largely constructed from spruce, birch and bamboo, covered with silk or fine linen and powered mostly by rubber, although with some steam, compressed air and CO_2 engines and even, from about 1908, an occasional petrol engine. Progress was very slow for some twenty years; however, national regulatory bodies were formed in several countries and the foundations of club movements and international competitions were laid. Model design virtually stagnated from around 1910 to the late 1920s but made rapid strides in the 1930s. Rubber was still the normal motive power although commercial miniature (10cc or ·60 cu. in.) petrol engines appeared in the USA in 1934 and radio control about three years later. Few engines were seen in Britain or Europe but towline gliders were developed and, during the war years, small compression-ignition motors were intro-

duced. In the US, the increasing losses of flyaway models arising from the wider use of petrol (gas) engines led to tethered flying which developed into control-line flying, steps which had been experimented with but not pursued in England in 1911 and 1924.

In the years following World War 2 there was another explosion of interest leading to introductions and developments which have brought aeromodelling to its present-day levels. Most of the progress relates to high performance aspects of flying with the introduction of high-tech materials and techniques, often at considerable expense, so much so that the vast majority of modellers have become vintage enthusiasts in order to put the fun element back into model flying. The term vintage is used loosely here, for while there are vintage fliers who abide by quite strict rules to ensure that their models are built exactly as the originals, most modellers just seek the simplicity associated with vintage-style designs. In England, the cut-off date for a vintage machine is December 1950, i.e. it must have been published or kitted prior to that date. The US cut-off is 1942 in general, but there are nostalgia classes for later dates and an old-timer category covering the early 1930s.

Average aeromodellers are likely to choose a design which attracts them, and which is straightforward and not too expensive to build. There are good arguments for choosing a kit model, especially for someone inexperienced or without a good model shop within easy reach, but a great deal can be learned from very simple models that anyone can make and, for very little extra trouble, there are designs published in magazines and books which can be built far more cheaply than the cost

A competition rubber model taking off from a specially-built platform. In 40 seconds it will be perhaps 700 ft. (say 210 m) high!

of an equivalent kit. However, before delving too deeply into construction let us categorise the various types of models.

MODEL CLASSES

Basically, there are three main groups of models — free flight, control line and radio control — and of these, free flight (F/F) is the most diverse. Each group subdivides with probably the simplest being control line.

Control-line models are always powered by a glowplug or diesel engine or, very rarely, by a petrol (ignition) engine or an electric motor. The model is attached by two wires to a handle held by the flier and thus flies round in a circle (actually within a hemisphere) with the flier turning continually to face the model. At the model end, the control wires are attached to lead-out wires permanently fitted to the model

and secured to a bellcrank. Thus the movement of the handle moves the bellcrank, which is connected to the model's elevators by a pushrod and horn; sometimes flaps are fitted to the wing trailing edge and a second pushrod operates these. As the model flies round, the flier has control over it in pitch — he can make it climb and dive and, if it has enough power, loop and perform horizontal or vertical figure eights. The flaps, if fitted, work in the opposite sense to the elevators and make manoeuvres smoother and tighter — they are only used on stunt models. Simple, light models can use fishing line for the control lines instead of wire, and line length can be anything from around 15ft. (5m) for a very small model to perhaps 90ft. (27m) for a large and powerful one. Wire can be single strand or up to seven strand, the multistrand being slightly easier to handle.

Fig. 1.1

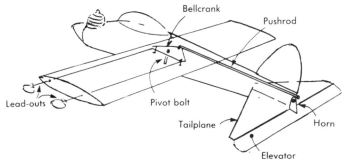

Bellcrank

Pushrod

Lead-outs

Pivot bolt

Tailplane

Horn

Elevator

A classic style control-line stunt model with wing flaps.
Right, 1994 World Champion combat flier Mervyn Jones with a
winning model.

There are several different sorts of C/L models – sport, stunt, speed, scale (which are self-descriptive), combat, carrier and team racer broadly covers them. Combat models fly two in a circle trailing paper streamers, each endeavouring to cut pieces off the other's streamer. Carrier involves a curved flight deck simulating an aircraft carrier for landing etc. and includes points for the difference between the model's fastest and slowest laps. Team racers fly three in a circle on a limited tank size so that refuelling stops are needed in races. There are various classes and offshoots such as Goodyear racing, rat racing, mouse racing etc., mostly American in origin and not frequently seen in Europe.

A beginner should start with a strong and easy-to-fly sport model. Points to remember are that the whole load of the model is taken on the bellcrank pivot bolt, which must be secure, and the control *must not* be stiff – the elevator control should move freely enough to drop under its own weight, or if the line tension slackens (because of wind) control of the model may be immediately lost. The fuel tank should feed from its outer rear corner, which should be level with the engine's spraybar, and the model's balance point should be slightly in front of the bellcrank pivot, which makes control simpler and means that the nose will tend to point outwards, helping to keep

the control lines taut. It is easier to fly from a take-off than a hand launch, especially if the launcher is inexperienced, which means that very short grass or a tarmac surface is needed. Always take-off downwind, since any breeze will help get the lines taut in the first half-lap, and keep the model low at first for maximum pull on the lines while you settle down.

Radio-control models can be of any type of aircraft but there is one immediate division – glider or powered. Taking the simpler first, gliders may be functional or scale and flown either from a flat site or on a slope. Those on a flat field are thermal soarers, relying on flying into rising air for long flights, having been launched by towline or bungee. A towline is a long line fitted with a ring which engages on the model's towhook; the flier runs with the other end of the line, or winds it onto a winch drum (often a converted hand-drill) fast enough for the model to climb out of an assistant's hands. When it has climbed as high as possible and settled to a gliding angle, slackening the line allows the ring to slip away, or a small pennant near the ring to pull it off. A bungee launch used to be carried out with elastic bungee cord, but nowadays plastic surgical tubing is used since it can stretch farther and catapults the model skyward in a much gentler and more consistent manner. Again the tow ring slips

Radio-controlled scale gliders are often big. This Minimoa by C. Williams spans 15 ft. 6 in. (4.77 m).

or is blown off the hook at the height of the launch, although a closed radio-operated towhook can be used. There is a class for hand-launched gliders, thrown javelin fashion and hoping to find rising currents at low level, and some experts use an electrically driven winch. Aerotows are possible but not used in competition.

Slope soarers are hand launched from near the top of a hill, escarpment or cliff and make use of the vertical component of wind blowing onto the face of the hill. The models can, of course, fly into thermal up-currents but need not rely on them for long flights. Different gliders perform better or worse depending on the wind strength. It is possible to see PSS models (power-scale soarers, which are scale models of full-size power aircraft built without engines for slope soaring), jets, airliners, fighters etc. all looking very realistic in flight (quite often fast flight!) and lacking only in noise.

Radio gliders are often quite large, 10–12ft. (3–3.5mm) being considered medium size. The smallest are rarely less than 5ft. (1.5m). The radio may control only the rudder, although more usually rudder and

elevators or ailerons and elevators. Three-function radio may use rudder/elevator/ailerons or two of these plus airbrakes. More channels or functions could be flaps, towhook and even a retracting take-off wheel.

Gliders will usually fly well with a small engine mounted on a pylon above the wing, or in the nose, which is used to climb the model gently to a height of several hundred feet, where there are good chances of

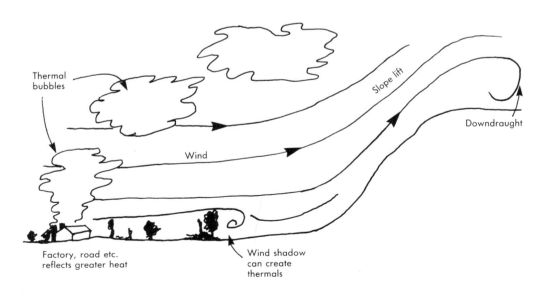

Thermal bubbles

Slope lift

Downdraught

Wind

Factory, road etc. reflects greater heat

Wind shadow can create thermals

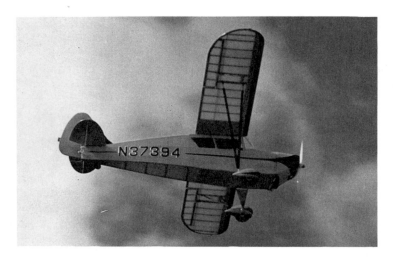

Left, American light planes of the 1930s, like this Interstate Cadet by Phillip Kent, are often chosen for first R/C scale subjects.

Below, trundling out a ¼ scale Sopwith Pup. World War 1 aircraft are popular R/C subjects at ¼, ⅓ and even ½ scale.

picking up thermal lift. This is one of the safest approaches for a beginner to learn to fly a radio-controlled model.

Powered R/C models come in all shapes and sizes, falling into one of three general categories — sport, aerobatic or scale. There is an aspect of speed, pylon racing, where three or four models race around a course marked by ground pylons but this is for experts only and should only be tackled by really experienced fliers. There is bound to be some blurring of classification since a scale model can well be fully aerobatic but flown for sport! It is possible to get some idea of a model's complexity by the number of radio channels (or functions) called for: single channel is rudder only, two means rudder/engine or rudder/elevator, three usually rudder, elevator, engine, four adds ailerons, five possibly retracting undercarriage or flaps and six both of these. Specialist functions (bomb dropping, parachutes, needle-valve adjustment etc.) can add channels almost infinitely. Some models use only ailerons instead of rudder for turn manoeuvres but most models designed as trainers have rudder, elevator and engine control, aileron trainers being considered the next step once the tyro has learned to fly.

Electric-powered R/C models are becoming more and more popular and efficient and can do virtually everything a glow- or

diesel-powered model can do. Again, for a beginner a powered glider is an excellent way to learn to fly, provided the instructions on charging the nickel-cadmium (nicad) cells are correctly followed.

There are also R/C helicopters, but these are the most difficult of all models to learn to fly, as well as being among the most expensive. If the challenge appeals to you, there are several books devoted to the subject and the wisest course is ask your public library to obtain one or two for you to study before choosing a model and radio.

Free-flight models offer enormous variety and only the main categories can be discussed here. The first division is power — rubber, glider, internal combustion (petrol or spark ignition, glowplug, diesel, four-stroke glow), electric, CO_2, compressed air — and each division breaks down into sport, scale and contest. There are competitions for scale models but reference to a contest (or competition) model normally relates to a purely functional machine designed for maximum performance and often of a shape or appearance quite strange to a newcomer.

Categories which are currently relatively minor or specialised are petrol (gas)

engines, four-strokes (seen quite normally in R/C models but not in F/F) and compressed air. The last, in modern form, uses a high quality plastic bottle pumped by a tyre pump to perhaps 7 bars (approx. 100 psi) driving a piston engine, also made substantially from plastic, for a minute or so, flying a 30–36in. (750–900m) model.

Rubber models are slightly handicapped by the absence of 'real' model shops, so not everyone can easily reach a shop selling rubber strip or ready-made propellers. However, there are mail-order sources which advertise most aeromodelling goods for those without a conventional stockist. Types range from 13in. span peanut scale and 8in. pistachio scale, usually flown in sports halls, to open rubber, usually 50–60 in. (1250–1550mm) wingspan and capable of 7 minute or longer flights. Most sport models are between 18in. and 36in. span (450–900mm) and the two major competition classes are Wakefield, 48–50in. (1250mm), now so high-tech that it is the province of only a handful in any country, and Coupe d'Hiver, around 30in. (750mm) or so and limited to 80 or 100gms of rubber. Vintage competitions attract vastly greater entries in many countries because pre-1950 models were, on the whole, simpler (and cheaper!), were (are) quicker

Above, small scale rubber models, available in kit form, may look simple but they are not suitable for first attempts.

Right, a streamliner with parasol wing dating from 1938. These elegant models are reproduced by keen vintage builders worldwide and are rewarding to build and fly.

to build and really much more fun to fly, at least for the average modeller.

Rubber strip is measured out, tied off and the ends bound under tension with knitting wool to make one large loop. This is then doubled etc. to the number of strands specified and the ends secured with rubber bands. The motor length is often as much as 1.5 times the distance from the propeller shaft hook to the rear anchorage point and the motor is braided by putting on turns before the last doubling, so that when the two ends are brought together the rubber intertwines to make a skein of the required length. The idea is to have the rubber hang between the hooks without uneven knotting or sagging to the fuselage floor, which could upset the model's gliding trim. Another way is to spring-load the propshaft so that

it moves forward as the tension comes off the unwinding rubber, bringing a spur into contact with a stop screwed into the nose-block. This method stops the propeller rotating before the rubber is fully unwound and since it stops in the same position every time, the stop can be placed so that the blade or blades of a folding prop always assume the same position, essential for a consistent trim. Alternatively, when the shaft is stopped a freewheeling mechanism automatically disengages and allows the propeller to windmill freely.

Most beginners make the mistake of choosing a scale model and, worse, a small one for their first attempt. Success is far more likely if a very simple functional model of at least 24in. (600m) span is chosen. Building and flying a rubber-powered model provides the best possible groundwork for future flying success.

Gliders are undoubtedly the cheapest way to start flying and perhaps the easiest to trim for good flights. However, a glider (or sailplane) needs to be towed up and the skill required to tow has to be learned. Some models are easier than others in this respect. Incidentally, at one time a glider was considered to be a machine that descended from its point of release, while a sailplane was capable of soaring higher after release. This was a carryover from full-size gliding, but with a greater understanding of how natural air movements can be used to prolong flight (q.v.) the terms have become effectively interchangeable.

Model gliders can be anything from paper-only to tiny balsa chuck gliders of perhaps 6–8in. span (150–200mm) and flown indoors, up to towline models usually limited (for competition) to a maximum of

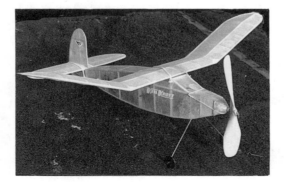

The Achilles is an excellent first choice for a beginner. It has been available for more than fifty years!

137in. (3.5m) and capable of very long flights off the standard towline length of 164ft. (50m). The line may be Terylene thread or, for bigger models, braided Terylene fishing line of about 25lb (11.5k) breaking strain; many experts use nylon monofilament but this has a tendency to tangle on the winch drum and is not recommended for beginners. Bungee launching for large gliders is possible using surgical tubing, while smaller models can be launched with a catapult line, usually consisting of three-quarters of its length normal towline and one-quarter length rubber strip as used for rubber models. The rubber does not have to be super strong — one strand

flights of 30–40 seconds or more. On a thermally day it is quite possible to lose them out of sight (o.o.s.) and flights of over half an hour have been timed. Contests usually count the best of three of nine flights.

Towline gliders are normally very efficient and sensitive to any slight lift, so that under good conditions a means of limiting the flight (a dethermaliser, explained later) is desirable to avoid a flyaway. They also use an auto-rudder, which is a simple device which helps to ensure a straight tow but allows the model to circle when it comes off the towline. Mostly it is just a length of thread tied between the towhook and a little horn on the rudder, which is held to

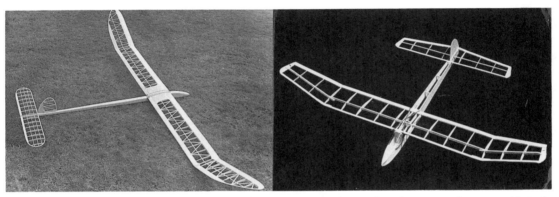

Two contrasting examples of gliders. That on the left is an A2 contest design of moderate complexity, notably in the anti-warp wing structure, while on the right is an example of real simplicity.

of ³⁄₁₆in × ¹⁄₃₀in. (5 × 1mm) usually being adequate to provide a gentle, steady climb to the full height obtainable with the length of line.

True catapult launching, using very strong or multiple strand rubber for a hand catapult, or made off to a peg fixed securely in the ground, can be dangerous for onlookers or passers-by since the model's initial speed can quite easily exceed 100 mph. It has to be strong which tends to make it heavy, and it is likely to have a pointed nose making a fairly lethal projectile. Care is needed.

Chuck gliders — officially hand launch or HL gliders — require to be thrown upwards at about 60 degrees and should make

one side to produce a turn by a thin rubber band. When the ring of the towline is slipped over the hook it pulls the thread forward, pulling the rudder central against a stop. When the rings slips off the rubber band pulls the rudder to its turn position. The main competition class of glider is the A2 (sometimes called Nordic) which is 6ft. or so (around 2m) span. There is a smaller A1 class which is by no means as popular. Open class gliders are most common and can be virtually any shape or size, although in some competitive events they are divided into below and above a certain wingspan, often 50in.

Power models. This term embraces a

very wide field, but basically it can be taken to mean any model fitted with an internal combustion engine. This may be *spark ignition* (often called petrol or gas motors) but relatively few are seen; *diesel*, more strictly compression ignition, running on ether/castor oil/paraffin or similar fuel, or *glowplug*, where the engine has a permanently glowing plug in the cylinder head and the fuel used is methyl alcohol (methanol) and castor oil, with possibly the addition of some nitro-methane. The glow is initially created by a low voltage battery but once running the heat of each combustion stroke ensures that the plug glows sufficiently to ignite the next and the battery may be disconnected. There are different oils and additives for various specialised purposes, as indeed there are with diesels. In the latter, ignition results from compression of the fuel/air mixture in the cylinder, the resultant temperature rise being sufficient to cause combustion. An adjustable contra-piston — effectively a cylinder head which can be moved up or down — controls the compression.

Two words, pylon and cabin, are used as shorthand for the two main types of model, but if a design does not clearly fit either general category, wing position may be used (high, shoulder, mid, low, parasol) followed by 'contest' or 'open cockpit' etc. Other less common labels may be used for unorthodox designs — delta, canard, pusher, ornithopter etc. A pylon model carries the wing well above the fuselage on what might be described as a forward fin; it bears little resemblance to any full-size aircraft but the configuration has proved the most efficient and reliable means of controlling the considerable power used in very high performance competition models, some of which can climb out of sight overhead in under half a minute. Cabin models bear some token similarity to full-size aircraft and, while they can have high performance, are more often seen in the hands of sport fliers.

Model sizes (for free flight) do not often exceed 8ft. span (2.5m), the most popular range being 3–5ft. (0.9–1.5m). Engine sizes are expressed in either cubic centimetres (cc) or cubic inches (cu. in.), 10cc being equivalent to 0.61cu. in., this being with rare exceptions, the largest size likely in F/F. The smallest commercially available are around 0.010cu. in. (0.16cc) but the smallest in popular use tend to be 0.75–1cc (·045–·061cu. in.) and in competitions 2.5cc (·15cu. in.) although these are broad generalisations.

Electric models are the major development story of the 1980s and 1990s, made possible by progress both in nickel-cadmium cells and permanent magnet motors. They can be quite small, perhaps 20in. (500mm) span, or any larger size you choose, and if fast recharge cells are used two or three minutes charge between flights is all that may be needed. Charging is often from a set of dry batteries or a car accumulator, although some enthusiasts have two or three sets of cells ready charged, each capable of giving several flights, so that all charging can be carried out at home. Most types and sizes of models can use electric power.

CO_2 motors, running on carbon dioxide charges from cylinders made for putting fizz into soft drinks, offer a quiet, clean and easy-starting source of power for small

Originally designed for free flight with a diesel of about ·75 cc, this Mam'selle is using electric power which gives clean and quiet flight.

models up to about 30in. (750mm) span, or larger if built lightly to fly indoors. Flights are rarely of extended duration but can be enjoyable in small fields in calm weather. The models really need to be lightly and neatly built, so a little experience with other types of models should perhaps be recommended. It is possible to adjust a motor's running time per charge to a long run at low power or a short run at high power and pro-rata, and it is not necessary to give a full charge, which is helpful when trimming.

Little has been said about scale models because although they are popular for radio, this book is concerned with basics and a newcomer to model flying should not attempt a scale model until reasonably experienced. This is due to the fact that scale models are more difficult to trim and are likely to sustain more damage if they hit the ground in the early stages. Since they are also more complex and take longer to build, repairs are likely to be more problematical. There *are* relatively simple scale models (of simple full-size aircraft) but so many beginners seem to want to tackle a Lancaster or a Spitfire!

Most scale gliders are large radio-controlled slope soarers, but there are one or two smallish free-flight designs based on military or semi-military machines. However, not all scale models are easy to tow up.

A Concorde free flight model which uses a tiny ·3 cc glow engine with a pusher propeller between the fins. The motor is almost invisible in flight.

A free-flight model Fieseler Storche, *an example of the high-wing layout most successful for F/F models.*

Scale rubber models are often quite small, but a jumbo rubber class (minimum span 40in. or 1m) began to attract a lot of interest around 1990. Most of the models are scaled-up vintage magazine or kit designs. Small kits should be avoided by beginners as they usually employ very small components and material sizes which need skill and experience to assemble satisfactorily.

Scale power models are, again, something to tackle once the novice has learned a reasonable amount about building and trimming for flight. They can often be less difficult than a rubber model since they have a constant source of power as opposed to the considerable initial burst of energy from a rubber motor; moreover the engine can usually be throttled down, or at least run on a very rich fuel mixture which slows it, to allow the trimming procedure to be carried out more cautiously. Never-theless, most experts are apprehensive when conducting initial flight trials with F/F scale models.

With radio, a power scale model of almost any subject can be flown in the hands of an expert flier. Learn to fly a trainer model on the same number of functions before risking a scale model. Most R/C clubs have one or two members prepared to give tuition and may actually have club trainers for new members to learn on, while one of the experts will take on flying a new model for a less experienced clubmate, trimming it out so that it is as safe as possible for the builder to fly. There are many trainers and sport type designs of scale-like appearance (but with the emphasis on docile flying characteristics) which offer a far better chance of success than being overly ambitious at the outset. It's often expressed as learning to walk before trying to run!

CHAPTER TWO

Tools and materials

For many years, the term 'model aircraft' immediately brought to mind balsa, but nowadays many models employ glass-fibre fuselages and veneered foam plastic wings, or incorporate vacuum-formed polystyrene parts and possibly high-tech materials such as carbon fibre, kevlar, boron etc. Covering used to be confined to fine silk or tissue, but now there is a wide choice of plastic films, some self-adhesive, and all capable of a degree of shrinkage by the application of heat. However, most of the sophistication relates to radio-controlled models and the basic home-built flying model is still a balsa frame covered with tissue or possibly nylon, although film coverings are becoming increasingly used.

Balsa is a fast-growing tropical timber mainly found in South America, notably Ecuador, but recently cultivated with some success in New Guinea. A tree grows to maturity in only six or seven years and is greatly affected by seasonal weather variation, chemical deposits in the soil, the position in which it is grown (e.g. on a dry hillside or in a damp hollow) and similar factors which have less obvious effects in slower-growing timber. Thus a tree may be full of faults and inconsistencies of hardness, weight and even colour, which makes selecting and cutting grades suitable for modelling quite difficult. Fortunately, many uses have been found for poorer quality wood which means that it is possible to buy top grade balsa at reasonable prices.

The wood is characterised by large, thin-walled cells interspersed with feeder channels and is full of sap when the tree is cut, though once dried out it is difficult to reintroduce moisture, except to a shallow depth on the surface, other than by prolonged submersion. When well damped,

flexibility is greatly increased but swelling occurs. A strip soaked for bending must be pinned to shape and allowed to dry out before cementing since the wet and dry lengths can show marked variation. For extreme flexibility soaking in ammonia will allow remarkable manipulation but again this must dry out before cement or glue is applied. In general it is preferable to use two or three thin strips laminated together round a former cut from thick card etc. rather than to try to bend one thick strip to shape.

Balsa varies considerably in weight from very light spongy material to the density of oak. For model use the weight per cubic foot may be quoted — 4—6lb for very light, often indoor, models or for soft block shapes such as engine cowls, 6—8lb for average sheet sizes, 8—10lb for stripwood (the smaller the harder) and for 'hard' sheet, and 10—12lb for hard strip. In fact, the budding builder soon learns to differentiate between grades by appearance, feel and 'bendability' to an adequate extent; it is claimed that experts tend to weigh each piece but older builders rely on experience.

There are two main cuts of balsa depending on how they relate to the growth rings of the tree. A sheet cut on a radius will be stiff and will split along the grain, while that cut on a tangent will bend relatively easily. Clearly, a component requiring stiffness, such as a wing rib or fuselage former, is best cut from a radial sheet while tangent-cut stock should be used for curved members such as wing upper surface sheeting, rolled tubes etc. The grain pattern of balsa is seldom very obvious but radial sheets tend to have narrow-spaced parallel lines of short grey or golden brown dashes and tangential sheets possibly a few broad

Fig. 2.1

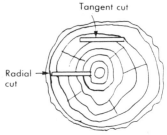

lines, widely spaced, only slightly different in shade from the basic colour, or really no visible pattern at all. Of course, there are many intermediate cuts falling between these two extremes but gentle pressure with a thumb against the fingers at the end of the sheet will easily indicate its degree of stiffness. Its weight is an indication of how hard it is likely to be, or an impression can be made with a thumbnail — medium hard will take an impression, hard will barely be marked, soft may have one or two surface fibres cracked — but don't make a habit of this with a shop's stock! Dampening a dent or impression in balsa will usually swell the fibres and remove the impression.

Balsa also varies in fibrous length, or stringiness for want of a better word, so that one strip may bend to a much greater degree than another of similar weight before snapping. Frequently one end of a strip bends more readily than the other,

TABLE 1.

Approximate Imperial/Metric Equivalents in Balsa Sizes

Inches	Millimetres
1/32	0.8
1/16	1.5
3/32	2.0
1/8	3
3/16	5
1/4	6
3/8	9
1/2	12
3/4	18
1	25.4

which can obviously affect say, the symmetry of a fuselage. Two simple checks are to pick up two strips by a forefinger at each end and press lightly, noting the curve each strip adopts, or to hold strips by their ends flat on a table edge with all but an inch or so overhanging and compare the droop. Reversing strip positions allows the best match to be made. For the most exact matching, strips should be cut sequentially from a sheet (after marking one end) but this sounds easier than it is in practice. Long fibre balsa is always preferable if a choice exists at the approximate weight required since it results in a stronger and more crash-proof model.

Balsa up to around 1/4in. (6mm) thick can be cut with a sharp bladed knife or scalpel unless it is very hard. No attempt should be made to force a cut in one stroke; several light cuts will achieve a better, less crushed result with a reduced danger of slipping. When cutting from sheet, always allow for the influence of grain and make the cuts in a direction which will make the grain steer the blade away from the component being cut rather than into it. Use a fretsaw for curves and a razor saw for straight cuts if the wood is hard or thicker than 1/4in. Never struggle to make a cut when the right tool would do it easily and never accept a faultily cut piece — scrap it and try again.

Glasspaper, or other abrasive material, is an essential either as a sheet wrapped around a block or glued to a strip of wood. It is better to cut just outside a line and then sand back to the line rather than risk cutting exactly on the line and then wandering inside it.

Hardwoods used for models are normally spruce, obeche and beech. Spruce is stronger and 'whippier' than balsa (it is also heavier), but is sometimes used for fuselage longerons or wing spars on larger models. If sheet material stronger than balsa is needed, obeche can be used although as thin ply is easily available this material is now encountered less frequently. Beech is the usual material for engine bearers and dowelling; it has considerable strength but is heavy. One other timber sometimes seen is jelutong, a very light smooth-grained wood sometimes used for carving rubber model propellers. Birch strip, at one time quite common in models, may be seen in dowel form and bamboo, once sold for modelling, is now only occasionally specified and must be split from garden canes. However, these do not seem to have the hardness and strength of the Tonkin type previously sold. Fine-toothed saws are best for cutting all sizes of hardwood.

Plywood usually comprises birch sheets laminated together in the thinner sizes useful for modelling, ranging from 1/64in. (0.4mm) to 1/8in. (3mm). Larger models may call for thicker ply, but the two most-used thicknesses are 1/32in. (0.8mm) and 1/16in. (1.5mm). Sometimes 3mm luan or gaboon ply can be used in place of birch as it is lighter but retains stiffness; this is the reddish coloured material often used on interior flush doors. All these sizes are three-ply — the number of plies is not an indicator of thickness and multi-plies are heavier (due to increased glue content) without offering any real advantage for modelling purposes.

Anything 1/16in. or thinner in ply can be cut with stout scissors, but always cut a good 1/16in outside the line — the remainder will trim off with a strong sharp knife-blade. This is much easier than cutting the whole piece with a knife in the first place. The best technique is to knife-cut all straight lines with the aid of a steel straight edge and use scissors for the curves, trimming to the final shape with a knife and glasspaper. A fretsaw can be used, but it is desirable to place a scrap piece of ply underneath the piece to be cut and cut through both otherwise the flex of the ply will snap the blades and may distort the cut. For anything thicker than 1/16in. a saw is necessary for both straights and curves.

Ply is much heavier than balsa and is used only at points of stress or where great strength is required. Typical examples are a dihedral keeper — a wing spar reinforcement at the point where the spar is cut to form a dihedral angle — or a forward former in the fuselage to which the undercarriage is attached and which may also carry engine bearers.

Wire as a basic material in modelling means steel piano wire, the best of which is hardened, tempered and plated. Up to the 1960s such wire would snap if an attempt was made to bend too tight an angle, but nowadays all that can be obtained in the USA or UK is much softer. This creates problems, particularly when used for propeller shafts on rubber models which have to run straight and true but which will bend if the model goes over on its nose on landing. This has led to competition fliers increasing the wire thickness over that previously used. When used for undercarriages the springiness is usually adequate but if overstressed, the wire may take a set so that after a heavy landing it may be necessary to straighten the assembly to its original position. It goes without saying that steel is heavy and the minimum of wire should be used.

Size measurement is quoted in Standard Wire Gauge (swg) which should not be confused with any other gauge. The accompanying table should prove helpful. Note that 16swg is 1/16in., a size only used on larger rubber models and small power jobs, and that the higher the number the thinner the wire. Single strand control-line wires are likely to be 33–38swg (the latter for very light models) and can be stainless steel or plain steel but not piano wire which is too springy and would prove difficult to handle.

Very little other metal is used in the average model except possibly small scraps of brass sheet or tinplate which may be used for bearings or freewheel devices, very thin aluminium sheet (e.g. some soft drink cans) for bendable hinge tabs and possibly heat shields for dethermaliser fuses, brass or aluminium tube for bushes etc. and small washers (usually tinplate hemispherical cup washers but also occasionally flat brass washers). There is also

WIRE/SHEET METAL GAUGES

British modellers refer to "piano wire" measured by Standard Wire Gauge, Americans by the term "music wire", usually expressed in inch decimals, although there is an official Music Wire Gauge. This table provides approximate equivalents, including metric (1mm = .0394in)

SWG	Inches	Inch fractions	Closest US Music Gauge	Millimetres (to Closest ¼mm
26	0.018	1/53	7	0.5
22	0.028	1/32	12	0.75
20	0.036	1/27	15	1
18	0.048	1/20	21	1.25
16	0.064	1/16	26	1.5
14	0.080	5/64	30	2
12	0.104	7/64	35	2.5
10	0.128	9/64	39	3.25
8	0.160	11/64	—	4

the possibility of an odd pin (perhaps made into a tiny eye e.g. to guide an auto-rudder line or simply acting as an anchor point for a rubber band) and, with a power model, nuts and bolts to secure the engine. You may also come across litho plate which is very thin aluminium alloy sheet used in some printing processes which, when salvaged and cleaned up, is widely used for cowlings etc. on scale power models. However, we are discussing basics rather than advanced techniques.

Plastics have only limited use in home-built models. Wheels and propellers moulded from various types of plastic materials may be bought, as may cockpit canopies and, for larger models, dummy engines and cowlings. However, apart from acetate sheet for cabin windows, the builder of a basic model is unlikely to make use of plastic. Modern covering products are frequently made from plastic films, but these and other materials used in covering are dealt with in a later chapter.

Adhesives are available in a quite bewildering variety but there are four main groups used in aeromodelling. In the very early days animal glues were used, as in carpentry, but with the advent of balsa, cellulose cements were introduced and became known as balsa cement. This is the first of the four groups. Drying times vary from make to make but it is recommended that non-stressed joints should be left for at least 1½ hours before handling — carefully — and that joints where any strain exists are allowed a minimum of 12 hours, the classic 'leave to dry overnight'. The cement is formulated to soak into a balsa surface and stronger joints can be achieved by lightly cementing both joint faces and allowing to dry for 20 minutes or so, then re-cementing and bringing the faces together. Very little pressure should be applied. The best joints are obtained when the joint faces are freshly cut and/or sanded so that there is no likelihood of any greasy dirt on the surfaces.

The second group consists of polymerised resins such as polyvinyl alcohol (PVA or white glue), aliphatic resins etc. and are relatively new on the scene having been introduced to modelling in the late 1970s. These glues are easy to apply and wash off fingers etc. easily with water before completely dry (as opposed to balsa cement which dries on fingers and has to be picked off!) but they need close-fitting joints and a degree of pressure while they dry. Non-stressed joints can usually be handled with care after 15–20 minutes but others need a minimum of 2 hours and are better left overnight.

Epoxy and similar two-part resins form the third group and in aircraft should be reserved only for very strong joints between dissimilar materials (e.g. metal to wood) or highly stressed areas since they are very heavy. They usually consist of two parts, resin and hardener, which have to be mixed very thoroughly immediately before use to form a thick, treacly paste which will bond almost any two grease-free surfaces with the exception of some plastics. Slight abrading of the surfaces with a file or glasspaper etc. ensures better adhesion. Setting time can be as little as five minutes but full strength develops over some hours, Always read the manufacturer's instructions with any adhesive as there are many variants; some resins are almost watery, others almost too stiff to mix, but thorough mixing is essential as are clean, dry, dust- and grease-free surfaces.

The fourth group are the cyano-acrylates, often termed superglues, but actually consisting of widely different products with differing viscosities, curing times etc. The virtually instant type is the most common in modelling, followed by glues which do not cure until a second component is sprayed on. Many react to common baking soda as a catalyst for immediate curing and most can be dissolved by glow fuel (methanol), so if you do get your fingers stuck . . . Some builders assemble complete models using no other adhesive, placing everything in position, applying drops of cyano to creep into every joint, then spraying with the setting agent. However, of all the glues mentioned, cyanos give off the most dangerous fumes, which if inhaled can cause irreversible damage so *they should always be used in conditions of proper ventilation.*

Of course there are other adhesives, some of which have particular applications e.g. contact adhesives, useful for laminating sheet materials; polystyrene cement for plastic card or moulded polystyrene parts; latex for veneering plastic foam shapes; rubber solution for covering sheeted surfaces with aluminium foil and various clear general-purpose glues such as tissue cements and pastes (see later) etc. However, initially at least, balsa cement or PVA will cope with everything needed for simple models.

Other materials used are mostly dopes, paints and other items related to covering and finishing discussed in Chapter 5.

TOOLS

One major advantage of building simple models is that very few tools are needed. As will be seen in Chapter 3, a modelling knife, glasspaper, a few pins and a tube of cement are all that is needed to make a chuck glider which will give hours of fun. Of

course, it is taken for granted that a pencil and ruler are available and that a small building board (e.g. a pastry board or similar) can be found. For more complex models rather more is needed but, compared with most hobbies, pastimes or sports it is still relatively little.

Any model will only be as true as its building board and the best procedure is to glue a piece of 10mm MDF (medium density fibreboard) to a completely flat piece of blockboard or chipboard. For models of up to approximately 50in. (1,250mm) span, a board 36 × 8in. (900 × 200mm) will prove adequate and with reasonable care will last for years. Apart from the lamination of two boards which helps to resist subsequent warping, the MDF takes pins readily. A separate small board should be used for cutting — this can be a piece of ply or a redundant breadboard or similar. For deluxe builders it can be topped with a self-healing cutting mat available from artists' suppliers, but this is not essential.

For cutting, many experienced modellers still use single-edge (backed) safety razor blades, although those available today are not as sharp as was once standard, nor do they hold their edges as well. Craft knives with replaceable blades are much more common as are surgical scalpels with interchangeable blades. These are sharp and should be treated with care; they can be re-sharpened on a fine stone. Always use a slicing movement, even when cutting through small square strip, and make a number of strokes rather than try to force a cut with heavy pressure. With sheet, cut down the grain rather than against it and be careful, if cutting on a wood board, that the grain of the cutting surface does not cause the blade to wander off-line on thin sheet. Always use a metal straight edge when cutting straight lines — even the back of a hacksaw will suffice. Alternatively find a metal merchant who may have inexpensive strip offcuts of approximately $\frac{1}{16}$ × 1½in. (1.5 × 40mm). Similarly, offcuts of MDF may be available from a building firm if a timber yard does not supply cut pieces.

A saw is needed when a part has to be cut down from something harder or thicker. Ideally a junior hacksaw, a fretsaw and a razor saw (like a miniature tenon saw) should be in the toolkit. These, plus perhaps a heavy duty DIY knife, should take care of just about everything. On very rare occasions a carpenter's tenon saw might prove useful, but most households have a few basic tools.

Hardened steel dressmakers' pins are usually used for the temporary pinning of structures, pushed in either by hand or by using a coin on the head, gripping the shank with pliers or, if necessary, tapping gently in with a light hammer. They can be withdrawn by twisting with pliers, especially if they are in contact with cement. If you do not have any pliers to hand, a steel pin can be gripped between two coins for removal. T-headed modelling pins may be used if preferred or alternatively glass-headed pins. However, beware of too much stress on the heads of the latter as the glass can shatter under pressure.

At least two pairs of pliers are needed — a heavy-duty pair which can be square-ended and a lighter taper-nose pair. Trying to bend piano wire with too light a pair rapidly ruins the pliers. Similarly, it is not possible for normal wire cutters, or pliers with wire-cutting features, to cut piano wire without themselves being damaged. Use the corner of an old file to nick the wire, when it will snap in the pliers. For anything thicker than 18swg, use a small vice for bending to obtain better results. Do not bend to too sharp an angle or the wire will crystallise and either snap or remain very weak. To solder such wire, clean it thoroughly with abrasive paper, immediately apply flux (Baker's Fluid or 'killed spirits of salts') and use a fair size iron, 50

or 60 watts or thereabouts, with plain tinman's solder. A copper, gas-heated bit of reasonable size can be used — often available cheaply from secondhand and surplus tool stalls in markets.

Desirable but not perhaps immediately essential is a hand drill plus a few small drills. The hand drill can also be used to wind rubber models!

Small files — round or rat-tail, triangular and warding or flat — have many uses. If the flat file is $\frac{1}{16}$in. thick it can be used for accurately notching components. A small electrical screwdriver and a slightly larger general purpose type are useful if they are kept in good condition, and small open-ended spanners, plus box spanners to fit two or three small sizes of nuts, should be acquired as the toolkit expands. A 'tool' which is essential and which should be used more than any other is glasspaper, or more properly garnet paper and/or carborundum paper in fine to very fine grades. Emery boards, as used in manicures, are helpful but a sheet of glasspaper pinned or glued to a foot length of 1 × 2in. batten will be found an asset throughout construction. Nothing shrieks 'beginner' more than a finished model which quite obviously wasn't carefully sanded to remove odd bumps and lumps and unintentional corners!

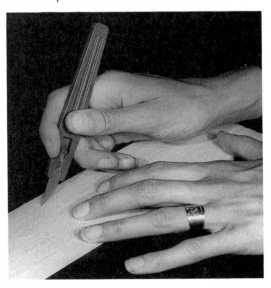

A basic tool is a sharp modelling knife or surgical scalpel. Remember not to use excessive force and that blunt blades lead to accidents.

In addition, you could invest in a razor plane, which is a small smoothing plane using double-edged razor blades. This is an example of a tool which some people — usually builders of bigger models — find invaluable and others never use at all. The same can be said for spray-guns, power tools, balsa strippers and a host of other items which are not required unless an obvious need arises. Buy only such tools as you need for the current project — you will soon find that your collection will build up. Remember too that a poor model can easily be made with good tools but it is much harder to make a good model with poor tools!

CHAPTER THREE

Paper and chuck gliders

It is surprising how much can be learned from the simplest of models at almost no cost. Take the paper gliders illustrated: a whole fleet can be made from two or three pages from an exercise book or a couple of A4 sheets of copy paper plus a cocktail stick or one or two matchsticks. Trace the one drawn using a fold in the paper at the bottom of the fuselage. You can trace it by pencilling over the lines on to a piece of kitchen greaseproof paper, then turning the tracing over, laying it accurately on the folded paper and going over the lines from the back with a pencil, which will transfer the first lines. The softer the pencil the better the lines will transfer. Alternatively, place a piece of carbon paper between the page and the folded paper — you must position the fold accurately. Or photocopy the drawing on a 'dry' copier, place the copy face down on the paper and rub a warm domestic iron over the back. You could, of course, simply make a copy and then fold it along the fuselage bottom line.

Yet another way is to hold the page against a window pane with the copy paper held on it — if the light is bright enough you will be able to see the lines through.

Having traced the shape, cut out the folded paper with scissors and accurately fold the wings and tail (follow the dotted lines). Note that on this model there is no fin and rudder, the flat fuselage and a small amount of V in the tail halves giving directional stability. Now cut about ½in. (12mm) of cocktail stick (or a slightly less length from a matchstick) and secure it in the nose fold, using only a trace of almost any adhesive or even a tiny scrap of adhesive tape.

Now check that the wings form a slight V (the dihedral angle) and have not become twisted with handling, then hold the model above your head, point it down vertically and just drop it. It should curve into a glide before it is halfway to the floor. The glide may be steep, indicating that there is too much weight in the nose, or it may be stally,

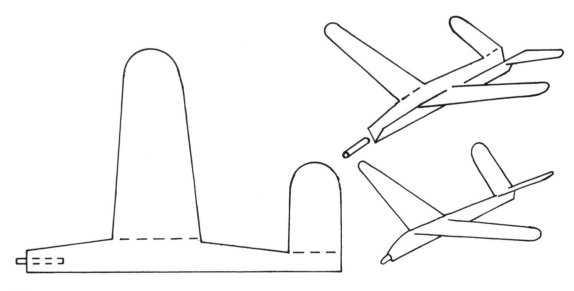

The completed model from the drawing opposite will easily fly 20–25 ft. (say 7 m) indoors.

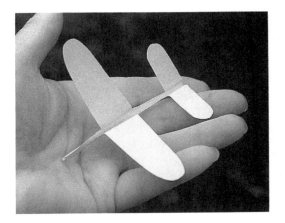

swooping up then dropping sharply before picking up speed and swooping up again, which means that more weight is needed in the nose. Either way, it will give you some idea of its speed, so for further flights you can hold it under the wing, point the nose slightly down and gently push it forward at about its flying speed, aiming at a point on the floor 10ft (3m) or so away. With any hand-launched model you must try to keep the fuselage at a constant angle and pointing slightly downward while swinging the arm forward to release the model at its flying speed. (The exceptions to this are nearly all highly powered competition models, but you won't be flying these at first!) The commonest faults are to try to throw the model and/or let its nose come up as the arm moves forward.

To adjust the glide of your paper model try either reducing the weight or adding a little more. You can also cut a second identical model but glue the weight slightly farther forward (if the first one stalled) or farther back; in the latter case the weight will be more than is needed and the model will fly faster than if the weight had been left where it was but with a little trimmed off it. Alternatively you can cure a dive by bending the trailing (back) edges of the tail halves equally upward, or the leading (front) edges of the wings upward. If the model flies straight and you want it to turn, put a little twist in one wing, raising the leading edge, which will give that wing a bit more lift than the other side and will therefore turn the model. You can, if you wish, put a small fore and aft cut on the trailing edges of the wings and tail so that you have a tab to bend up or down. This will effectively give the model ailerons (on the wings) and elevators (on the tailplane).

In order to achieve a more conventional aircraft appearance, a separate rudder can be cut and fitted in the fold at the tail end. Although the paper will not weigh much there is a danger that the adhesive might, so be sparing with it and remember to compensate at the nose end. A biplane may be made by cutting a long thin wing and folding it, trapping the fold in the fold of the original shape. Many variations are possible including seagulls, canards and deltas, all of which can be made to fly well, and while you are experimenting you will subconsciously be recording data which you can draw on for later, more complex models. Try competing with friends – launch while standing on a step-ladder and see whose model travels the farthest!

Examples of paper models, including a dragon, a seagull and a biplane. All fly well.

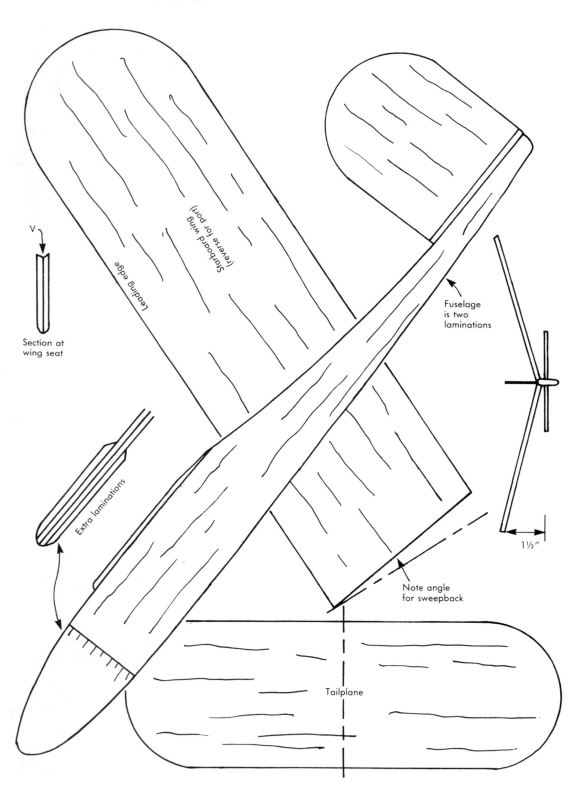

V

Section at
wing seat

Leading edge

Starboard wing
(reverse for port)

Extra laminations

Fuselage
is two
laminations

1½″

Note angle
for sweepback

Tailplane

The next simplest model is a chuck glider, or hand-launched glider to give it its official title. This is the other exception to launching downward at flying speed — a chuck glider is thrown upward as hard as possible, usually at a 60 degree angle and banked over at 60 degrees. An average flight for a beginner will probably be between 10 and 20 seconds. This may not sound very long but just sit and watch the second hand of a clock or watch and think of a model in the air for that length of time. On a good 'thermally' day flights of over a minute are not uncommon and a surprising number of these simple aircraft do in fact fly out of sight, often upwards, when there is good lift about.

The drawings are shown full-size for a very simple example of a chuck glider. The wing, tail and rudder tips are all semi-circular so you can draw the pieces on a sheet of $\frac{1}{16}$in. (1.5mm) moderately soft balsa if you prefer rather than trace them, though you will need to trace the fuselage. This is made up of two identical pieces cemented together, so having marked and cut one, it can be used as a template to cut the second. These two pieces should be cut from the hardest part of the sheet if there is any obvious variation. Cement them together and leave them to dry on a flat

surface under light pressure — put a piece of flat wood on top and then a book on top of that.

Cut the wings and tail pieces and sand them with fine glasspaper. Both the wings and tail will benefit from having the leading edges rounded and the trailing edges thinned slightly. Do this by holding each piece on a flat sheet of timber with the trailing edge flush with the timber's edge then sand gently with the paper on a block of wood, using strokes along the grain but angling towards the edge. Sanding balsa creates a lot of dust so it would be wise to either sand out of doors or in the garage rather than indoors. You will notice that the centre ends of the wing halves are slightly angled, so that when they are cemented together they will have what is called sweepback. This is an aid to stability which can be used to retain the same stability as a straight wing would give while allowing a slight reduction in dihedral angle and hence a small increase in lift efficiency. Sand a very slight bevel on each centre end, re-membering that one wing is left and the other right, and run a thin line of cement along each and put aside to dry.

When the fuselage is dry, sand around the outline to ensure that both parts are flush, then mark the wing and tail positions.

The finished chuck glider from the drawings opposite. It will teach construction and trimming lessons as well as being fun to fly.

23

Carefully excavate a shallow V where the wing will sit using a pointed knife-blade or the corner of a razor blade — but keep your fingers out of the way! Now cut the two extra nose pieces and cement in place, holding with a clothes peg until dry. Round off all the corners except at the wing and tail seats. Place one wing panel on a flat board and lightly weight it to prevent it moving too easily and slide a strip of kitchen film (or waxed paper), or thin polythene (from a food bag etc.) under the straight end. Cement the end of the other wing and fit in place, blocking the tip up 3in. (76mm) and using two pins at the joint end to ensure contact while the cement dries. Also at this time cement the fin to the tailplane, ensuring that is exactly at right-angles.

When dry, set the fuselage vertical on the board and press a pin into the board each side to hold it vertical, without pinning through it. Cement the tailplane in place, packing loosely under each tip to ensure that it is parallel to the board; a couple of temporary pins can be pushed in to make sure it doesn't move. Cement the wing in place, using books or tins to pack under the tips to hold them at an equal height from the board, and again pin temporarily to the fuselage. Sight from each end to check that the wings are properly aligned and that the tailplane and fin are truly square and in alignment. Also sight from above to make sure that the wing and tail are squarely placed. This true alignment is very important. Leave to dry out thoroughly then add a thin fillet of cement along the joints between the wing and fuselage, and the tail and fuselage and again leave to dry. Be patient!

Check the model all over. You can, if you wish, give it a coat of sanding sealer, banana oil or clear non-shrinking dope, leave to dry then sand all over with very fine carborundum paper; these are all akin to a coat of cellulose 'varnish' to strengthen and waterproof the balsa surface. Now push several panel pins into the thickened part of the nose, or drill a couple of holes along it and push in bits of cored solder, until the model balances slightly nose-down when supported by a fingertip in the centre of each wingtip.

Traditionally, all models are supposed to be test-glided over long grass, because obviously grass will cushion the arrival of a model which fails to fly properly at first. This is not so important with a chuck glider although it will certainly last longer if it is flown over grass rather than tarmac or gravel. For the first tests, hold the model with a finger and thumb beneath the wing trailing edge, point the nose slightly downward and launch smoothly and gently, looking at a spot approximately 25–30ft in front. The action is rather like throwing a dart but is not as hard, the aim being to release the model at its normal flying speed. Naturally this has to be a guess at first but will become easier with practice.

As has already been mentioned with the paper model the glide may be steep — even as much as a dive — or it may climb, stall, drop to recover flying speed then climb again and repeat the sequence. You may be lucky enough to achieve a nice smooth glide straight away. To correct too steep a glide it will be necessary to remove a pin or piece of solder, for a stally flight add a pin and try again. When you have achieved what

Fig. 3.1

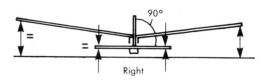

Right

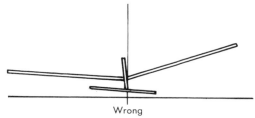

Wrong

A high-tech chuck glider equipped with a carbon-fibre boom and a dethermaliser (q.v.).

appears to be a reasonable glide path, you can launch the model harder, pointing it slightly upwards and slightly banked. Watch what happens and check whether the same thing occurs on every flight, adding or removing a pin as appropriate.

If the model is launched at moderate speed upwards without banking it, it will probably stall and may well drop straight to the ground without resuming gliding flight. The reason for this is that both the wing and tail are mounted flat on the fuselage, i.e. neither has an angle of incidence. A normal aircraft has the wing set at a slight angle, perhaps 2–3 degrees on the average model, with the tailplane at zero angle — this arrangement helps stability in pitch. It means that if the aircraft is disturbed from its normal flight path, a force arises which will tend to restore normal flight. However, if the aircraft's speed is increased dramatically, the difference in angles produces a tendency to loop. Clearly, a chuck glider which is thrown much faster than its normal flying speed cannot have an incidence difference or it would simply loop every time it was launched hard. It follows therefore, that its pitch stability is marginal and it must be flown in such a way to prevent it getting into a critical position. Banking the model on a launch turns any looping tendency into a spiral climb, enabling it to slide into a glide without stalling. You may well be surprised at how far the model will fly from a good hard launch once you have got its trim right.

CHAPTER FOUR

Traditional construction

In modern parlance, traditional construction means tissue-covered balsa framework, sometimes referred to as 'stick and tissue' modelling. For free-flight models the method has much to commend it, notably light weight, moderate cost, easy repairability, modest tool requirements etc. and it has immense value in teaching dexterity, structural analysis, patience and commonsense to list but a few of its characteristics. A present-day complication is the switch from imperial measurement to metric, as most of the plans available are expressed in inches and young potential modellers more familiar with millimetres may find it difficult dealing with inch fractions. Some balsa is now cut in metric sizes but most (at the time of writing) is still in inches. Further problems arise due to the fact that America still works in inches and if Britain goes entirely metric the fruitful interchange which has always existed between US and UK modellers will become more difficult. It seems sensible, therefore, to list equivalent wood sizes at the outset.

A majority of fuselages for models are what is known as *slabsiders*, meaning substantially square or rectangular in cross-section as opposed to *streamliners* which are most often round or elliptical in section. There are, of course, intermediate shapes, usually in the form of a slabsider box carrying a shaped turtle deck on top and/or bottom, achieved by adding light formers and stringers to the basic box. Sometimes this curved addition is confined only to the nose of the fuselage, for appearance or perhaps to gain a slight aerodynamic advantage by streamlining the part of the structure which first encounters the airflow.

The basic box fuselage is built with four fore and aft strips called *longerons*, held in place by vertical spacers to make two sides joined by cross-spacers top and bottom. Working drawings for building such a structure show a side view over which the sides are assembled, and a top view on which the sides are erected. This top view shows the same longerons viewed from above as those seen from the side in the side view; quite a number of new builders have built two sides and then a separate top and bottom, ending up with eight longerons instead of four! This sort of fuselage may have bulkheads (solid sheet cross members) or formers; a bulkhead carries further structure such as engine bearers in a power model, whereas a former is concerned with the external shape and therefore frequently has its centre cut away to save weight. As ever, there are borderline cases as with a bulkhead fitted to carry the undercarriage in a rubber model which has to have its centre cut away to pass the rubber motor, which one draughtsman will call the *u/c bulkhead* and another the *u/c former*.

To build a slabsider fuselage, the longerons are placed over the drawing and held in place with pins pushed in either side of the strip. Pins pushed through will weaken the finished structure. It is usual to cover the plan with kitchen film or grease-proof paper to prevent excess adhesive sticking the structure to the drawing. Alternatively rub the site of every joint on the plan with a candle or a dry bar of soap. Strong curves in longerons may entail steaming or soaking the strips, pinning them down and allowing them to dry out before cementing in the spacers. A piece of light metal tube taped to the spout of an old kettle makes a suitable steam box. Slip the wood strips into the tube and boil the kettle for two or three minutes. The tube will have to be supported in some way and it gets quite warm so it might be easier to wet the strips with hot water, leave them to soak for a few minutes then gently bend them, re-soaking if necessary. The wood swells and lengthens, returning to dry size as it dries out, so that it is inadvisable to stick it wet. A severe curve should be made by laminating strips, e.g. two $\frac{1}{16}$in. × $\frac{1}{8}$in. on edge will curve easily and equal $\frac{1}{8}$in. square when cemented together.

Some modellers cut pairs of spacers before pinning the longerons. others cut them to fit as they go along. Again, some will build one side complete then lay the other longerons on top and build the second side, while others pin all four longerons and build both sides simultaneously. In both cases the aim is to ensure that both sides are identical and unless pieces of greaseproof paper have been laid on the first side joints before adding the second, the two sides will lift as one and will need to be separated by working a thin blade between them. This is one occasion when, with care, a double-sided razor blade is useful since it can be worked between spacers as well as between longerons, attacking a stubborn unwanted joint from all round.

It is possible to cut a pair of temporary card formers to help assemble the sides together, pushing them out once the main cross-spacers are firmly in place. Alternatively, place the sides over the drawing

Fig. 4.1

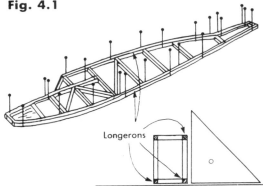

Longerons

with pins each side, then pass a not-too-tight rubber band over them, hooking it to drawing pins set two to three inches away either side. Cement in the first pair of spacers, top and bottom, and check that the sides are vertical using a set-square. The rubber band can be biased to move the sides until all is square. Initially, either cement the widest pair of spacers and the tail end or the two widest pairs of spacers, in which case make sure that the nose and tail ends coincide by holding a square to them. Once two pairs of spacers are in place, leave to dry. Positioning the others is then quite simple, using light rubber bands where necessary.

In many designs there may be diagonals between vertical spacers and these should be put in as the sides are built, since often they brace the structure against the spring

Fig. 4.1 (above) shows one side of a typical cabin model and indicates where pins might be placed.

A simple slabsider fuselage for a rubber model.

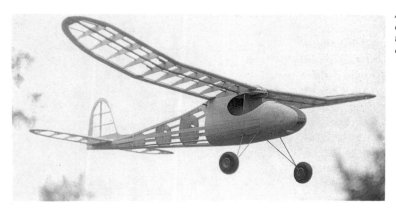

A multi-stringered fuselage built on a crutch is a feature of this 45 in. free-flight power model by the author.

of a curved part. For example, a body with a straight top longeron but a strongly curved lower one will change shape when it is unpinned, putting a bend in what should be the straight top and flattening some of the curve from the bottom. Strategically placed diagonals will prevent this from happening and they may also brace a joint which may take a load, e.g. where the undercarriage enters the fuselage. In a lot of designs there may be inset sheeted bays, for example at the nose where a lot of handling may be expected. These filler panels should also be inserted before unpinning the structure, and often the best method is to lay a piece of paper over the bay and run a finger round, making an impression of the inside corners of the longerons and spacers. This paper can then be cut and checked, then used as a template for cutting a piece of sheet.

Streamline fuselages cannot be built flat in the same way, though one technique is to build two halves, usually left and right, and join them. If the drawing does not show two halves, one can be built and removed and the appropriate area of the plan lightly damped with thin oil or paraffin etc. which will render it sufficiently transparent for the second half to be built on the back of the plan. A better (and less smelly!) idea is to lay carbon paper face up under the plan and go over the required lines on the right side, thus transferring them to the back of the plan. For a circular fuselage, or a two-

piece one to be made as a top and bottom section, one view is of course adequate.

Other methods include building a crutch with temporary spacers, allowing formers to be positioned on the crutch and the spacers to be removed once a few stringers have been cemented in, or a jig arrangement. In the latter, the formers all have a square hole cut on the datum line, the centres having been cut out and temporarily tack-cemented back in place. They are then threaded on to a square piece of timber — the jig — and held with pins in their true places. Once a few stringers have been added the pins can be removed, and when all the stringers are positioned and dry, the jig can be withdrawn and the former centres removed by wiggling a blade through between stringers. A further method which emulates full-size techniques is to build a box fuselage and add formers to the sides, top and bottom. This tends to produce a slightly heavier structure overall, but is frequently used for scale models.

Formers do not have to be cut from sheet in every case. Where a circular or oval functional fuselage is required, it is common to use what are termed *wound formers* made by laminating narrow strips of thin sheet balsa. The thickness has first to be decided, say three laminations of $\frac{1}{32}$in. (0.8mm) balsa, and a tracing made of a section, then a line drawn, in this case $\frac{3}{32}$in. (2.4mm) inside the section outline. This is transferred to hardboard or cheap

Sheet balsa fuselage construction is often found with slim, rectangular glider fuselages and on some power models.

ply and cut out to form a *mould* or *shadow*. A strip of balsa is cut from a suitable sheet, perhaps ⅛in. or ³⁄₁₆in. (3 or 4.5mm) wide, and wound round the mould, cementing the overlap as it goes. It is best to pin the mould down over a piece of greaseproof paper or plastic film. This is repeated for each former.

Where stringers are notched into a former cut from sheet and subsequently tissue (or other) covered and shrunk, the edges of the former between the stringers show up rather badly, giving what is called a 'starved horse' appearance. In most cases the edges can be scalloped away between the stringers or the former cut undersize by the thickness of the stringers and the stringers then cemented on the outside of the former. Naturally, where there are places where the former should reach the surface, such as for mounting an undercarriage or flying surfaces etc., this can be allowed for in its shape, or a small piece of stringer-thickness sheet, cut across the grain, can be cemented in. This not only brings the former to the surface but also provides a slightly wider support for the covering at that point, improving the finished appearance and providing strength where needed.

One other type of fuselage should be mentioned — the *diamond*. This is really just a square, completely symmetrical body turned on its corner, one theory behind it being that if the airflow is not parallel with its centre-line, presenting a corner rather than a flat surface to it results in reduced drag. Certainly diamonds have proved very competitive and are thought by some to be a halfway stage between slabsiders and streamliners, having the ease of construction of the former with the notionally better aerodynamics of the latter but without the weight. One small drawback is the increased complexity of the wing mounting; most often this is a parasol style using bamboo or hard balsa runners on a wire cabane. The extra drag of the wires etc. is probably offset by the whole wing working, in a superior envelope too, but we need not go too far into that!

WINGS

Apart from solid sheet wings on small models such as the glider in the last chapter or the little rubber-powered models that can be bought ready-to-fly, wings have always consisted of a framework of ribs and spars covered by some light material. On early models, single surface wings were common — the ribs were usually birch strip steamed to shape with a fabric covering on the top surface only. Such wings are still to be found on ultra-light models flown indoors (although the ribs are cut from sheet balsa and the covering is very lightweight tissue or possibly microfilm) or, as would be expected, on reproductions of vintage models. However, over the last 50–60 years, most wings have been double-surfaced, having

29

reasonable thickness and being covered, usually with tissue, top and bottom. There are wide differences in the actual wing section (rib shape) and spar arrangement, all of which have points for and against; one of the joys of modelling is that there are so many variables! Incidentally, in aerodynamic language any surface capable of lifting is an aerofoil and its cross-section is an aerofoil section — the same as wing section — but common usage now seems to use 'aerofoil' (airfoil in the USA) to mean the section shape rather than the whole surface.

A simple conventional wing will usually have a leading edge, a mainspar and a trailing edge, the mainspar generally being placed at the point of greatest depth of the section — this is likely to be at about one-third chord back. As you will gather, chord is the overall front-to-back width of the wing. There might be a rear spar or subsidiary small spars. Spar placing has to relate to where the strength is needed and also how the pull exerted by shrinkage of the covering will affect the structure. Because wings are large thinnish areas and need to be kept light, they can warp fairly easily and warps tend to have significant effects on how the model will fly, so spars need to be arranged to minimise the chances of warping or to ensure that any warp that might occur will at least tend to beneficial effects rather than the reverse.

Larger wings bear larger loads but spars cannot be increased in size without incurring weight penalties, so methods of increasing structural efficiency must be employed. If instead of having one solid mainspar the same weight of wood can be split in two, one piece can be used on the bottom surface and the other immediately above it on the top, i.e. one piece in tension and one in compression for up and down loads. The result is a considerable increase in strength and stiffness which can be further boosted for only a small weight penalty by webbing between the two spars with thin sheet panels between the ribs. Further strength

will result from cutting the webs with the grain vertical. If the forward part of the wing is sheeted top and bottom between the leading edge and the mainspar, this gives a D-box which offers enormous strength and rigidity with the additional advantage of accurately maintaining the aerofoil section in its most crucial area. In fact, sheeting the top surface only will provide most of the advantages, saving the weight of wood and glue which otherwise would be used to sheet underneath.

The region most likely to warp is where the wing is thinner, which also happens to be the largest unsupported area. Any subsidiary spar must necessarily be shallow because the section is thin and therefore likely to warp with the wing. Methods of minimising warping include capping the ribs by sticking a thin strip top and bottom, turning them into I-section members, using diagonal ribs rather than (or as well as) fore and aft ones, or using diagonal bracing between the ribs. Full geodetic construction produces an excellent warp-free result but is complex and time-consuming.

Warping is used deliberately to produce particular flight patterns and expressions such as *wash-in* and *wash-out* will be encountered. Wash-in is progressive *in*crease in incidence angle towards the tip, wash-out is a *de*crease in angle. If the wing on one side of a model has wash-in, that wing will lift more than the other, so the model will be banked and will turn away from the washed-in tip, and so on. Wash-out is most commonly used, to slow down stalling (breakdown of lift) at the wingtip. The slight angular changes needed are obtained by packing the appropriate part of the wing when it is pinned down for the covering to be shrunk, but it can subsequently be introduced or modified by the application of heat and/or damp.

Packing is usually needed when constructing a wing since the leading edge on most sections is unlikely to be flat on the building board and it will, therefore, require to be packed up into position with scraps of wood at regular intervals. The curve of an aerofoil section is called *camber* and the underside, on most simple models, is flat but on many other models forms a hollow curve called *undercamber*. Usually there is a light spar at the highest point of the concave curve to help attach the covering, and this spar too will need to be packed into position during construction. With undercamber, the trailing edge member is unlikely to be flat on the board so the front edge of this will also need to be packed up. Leading and trailing edge timber is generally available pre-formed which saves a lot of awkward shaping. That said, one shape of leading edge cannot accurately fit a whole range of sections, so experts or perfectionists will shape their own. The trailing edge is less critical and, being thinner, is inclined to curve if sanded more on one face than the other so is generally bought ready-shaped.

Ribs are usually cut from sheet balsa and the favoured choice is a constant chord wing where every rib is the same size. If the basic rib is traced onto thin ply, or even thin aluminium sheet, it can be used as a template to be laid on the balsa and cut round. Some modellers prefer to draw round it with a ballpoint pen, drawing all the ribs then cutting round all the lines. The resulting ribs should then be neatly stacked and pinned together (usually two pins pushed in from each side of the stack) and lightly sanded to match. Often it is best to leave

cutting the spar notches until this stage is reached, ensuring that the ends are flush then using a saw and file to cut the notches in the stack.

Tapered wing ribs are more difficult. Templates for the largest and the smallest rib (on the straight tapered section) should be cut, then rectangles of sheet sandwiched between them, cut and sanded to match, followed by cutting the notches. The process should then be repeated with the templates reversed for the other wing half. The alternative is to plot each rib, or trace each one if they are all given on the drawing from which you are working. These latter remarks also apply to odd-shaped wings such as ellipses or bird-type wings. It is sometimes possible to use the top outline of a template to produce different length ribs if the length is marked on the balsa, plus the l.e. and t.e. depths and the mainspar position and depth. The template can be swung to engage with these marks but not if there are great differences in length and depth. Another approach is to calculate the percentage length change and reproduce the basic rib on an enlarging/reducing photocopier, which also has the advantage of being transferable onto balsa as previously outlined.

At one time there was a vogue for 'sliced' ribs, where a separate top and bottom are used, both being of constant depth. A piece of sheet is cut to the chord width and the

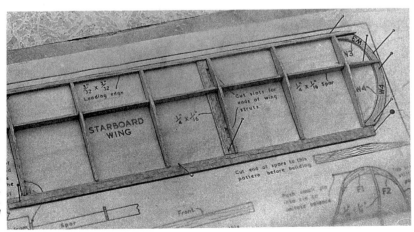

A simple wing on the building board. It uses a single mainspar and cut sheet tip and is part of the kit model shown on page 7.

ribs sliced off by moving a template down approximately ⅛in. at a time. The slices can then be cut to length to fit a gently tapered planform. One result is that the overall depth of the ribs as a percentage of the chord will gradually increase as the chord decreases, but provided the taper is not too great this may not be unacceptable.

To build a wing, one flat panel at a time should be tackled. The suggestion 'build the wing flat, then crack and cement at dihedral breaks' is common but misleading since there is bound to be a difference in length of spars depending on their positions. Imagine a wing ¾in. thick built flat. When 'cracked' to, say 10 degrees dihedral angle, the top surface loses over ⅛in. in length, so if there are several spars they will all require to be different lengths. It is therefore better to build one panel and, when dry, prop it firmly in position at the correct angle and build the second panel onto it etc. An even better idea, where a reasonably deep mainspar is used, is to 'build' the spar first, complete with any dihedral braces specified, which will ensure correct angles as each panel is built to the spar.

Care should be taken that the rib notches are a good fit on the spars. Too tight a fit on a lower spar will wedge the notch further open, distorting the ends of the ribs upward, too loose a fit will mean a bigger blob of cement or glue adding weight and also on drying, shrinking, pulling in the sides of the notch which forces the rib ends downwards. It is normal simply to butt the ribs against the leading edge (but make sure they all touch and are properly stuck) because this is usually fairly deep, although if it is substantial a shallow notch put in with a file of the same thickness as the rib makes a much stronger joint. The trailing edge, being thinner and wider, is almost always notched to receive the ribs, except perhaps on smaller models.

Take precautions against the structure becoming stuck to the plan, especially on long joints such as often occur between the trailing edge and a curved tip member cut from sheet. In many instances in larger models, the centre section ribs are reduced in depth to receive sheet covering (which brings them back up to normal depth) and this should be partly carried out on the top surface, while the centre section is pinned flat on the board, to minimise the chance of a warp creeping in. A warped centre section is not always easy to spot but has considerable effect on flight. A lot of designers show little triangular gussets in stressed areas or at the rib ends where they are thinnest, along the t.e. All of these can be cut ready, then cemented in in the air, so to speak, but only one panel at a time and the panel pinned back down for approximately an hour. Gussets will be stiffer and stronger if the grain is parallel to the hypotenuse, cut as sketched.

Always check the wing carefully, particularly the joints. Sand it well, particularly where the ribs meet the l.e. and t.e. If they project even slightly above or below, a wrinkle will appear in the subsequent covering. Try to blend everything in smoothly, using fine glasspaper. Not only will the model look infinitely better but its performance will be improved.

Wing for a 60 in. (1.5 m) power model using top and bottom members for both main and subsidiary spar. Ribs are notched into both l.e. and t.e.

Fig. 4.2

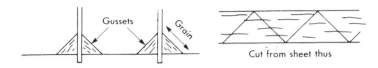

Gussets Grain

Cut from sheet thus

TAIL SURFACES

In essence, these may be treated as small wings but, as they are smaller, lighter and thinner than wings, it is even more important to ensure that they are warp-free. Quite possibly they may have symmetrical sections, meaning that both leading and trailing edges need to be packed off the building board.

Where a movable control surface is built in, for example a rudder or trim tab on a fin, it is best to build the whole thing as one piece and cut through outlines etc. to free the tab. For free flight, the tab (or rudder) is likely to require to be set to an angle which it will hold permanently once established and a 'hinge' of aluminium, soft iron or copper wire is used, normally just two short pieces pushed and cemented into holes pierced appropriately in the meeting edges. An alternative is two tiny pieces of thin aluminium sheet cut from a drinks can or something similar, cemented into slits made by a sharply pointed knife-blade. The tab is bent as necessary during trimming and lightly secured with cement when the required angle is found. Flexible hinges for mobile controls can be made from tape or sewn thread as sketched or proprietary hinges can be purchased.

UNDERCARRIAGES

There are really only two materials used on the average u/c — piano wire and bamboo. Most small models with a u/c have a simple wire one fixed in place, frequently between two narrow sheets of balsa cemented vertically across the bottom of the fuselage. Wire is also used for larger models, but bamboo may also be used and the u/c legs are usually detachable, plugging into tubes bound into the fuselage. Power models again are usually found with fixed wire undercarriages, the wire(s) being secured to one or more ply bulkheads either by sewing through pre-drilled holes with strong thread or thin wire or by means of J-bolts or small plastic saddles bolted over the wire. Often the spring in a single cantilever wire leg each side is adequate, although for larger and heavier models a double leg each side is common, the wires being brought together just above the axle, bound with florists' wire or similar and soldered together.

The tubes used for detachable legs are usually of brass but may be aluminium, depending on the size and weight of the model, held in place by binding or sewing, or wrapping with a tissue strip, cement then being rubbed in, or secured to a sheet part

Fig. 4.3

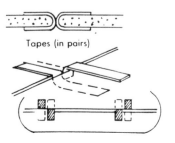

Tapes (in pairs)

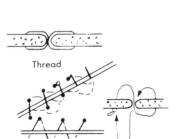

Thread

Diagonally-set ribs forming a Warren girder type structure are often used on tailplanes because they tend to reduce warping.

of the body with a silk or nylon patch cemented over and further cement rubbed in. In the case of detachable cantilever bamboo legs they may simply plug straight into card or wound gummed paper tubes set at the appropriate angle in the body, exiting through sheet balsa panels and firmly cemented to a strong point at the top.

Bamboo legs may have a wire L at the top to plug into a horizontal tube, one at the bottom, to provide an axle, and a wire spring against which they can pivot, the top of which also plugs into a tube. This is fairly common on vintage models. The wire may be attached to the bamboo by binding with thread, but in order to prevent it from twisting in the binding it must either be doubled back for a short distance, the end turned over and cut off short, locating in a hole burned in the bamboo with a hot needle, or the end of the wire flattened on some sort of anvil with hammer blows; heating the short bit to be flattened makes this quite easy.

Wheels are best held between tiny washers soldered to the axle. Fixing the first washer is easy with no wheel present, but once the wheel is on, a piece of wet newspaper should be laid over it, the washer slipped on and the soldering carried out quickly with a very hot iron. The paper can then be torn away and oil introduced to counter any flux that may have run along the axle and might later cause the wheel to

Clothes pegs make useful clamps. Here a dihedral joint is being made, the pegs applying pressure to braces while the cement dries.

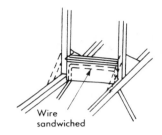

Wire
sandwiched

Fig. 4.4

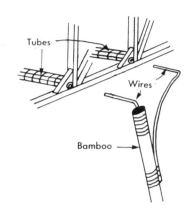

Tubes

Wires

Bamboo

seize. It is possible to use tiny curls of thin copper wire instead of washers or, for larger diameter axles, collets or screw-spring wheel retainers can be bought. For very small models, roughen the end of the axle and put a turn or two of cotton in place with a little blob of cement.

The wheels themselves can be bought although for rubber models it is not difficult to make a pair. Two circles cut from balsa sheet and cemented cross-grain form the basis, but it is easier to cement them each side of a thin ply disc. If a compass is used to mark them out the centre hole can be opened out and a 10BA bolt passed through.

This can then be held in a hand-drill chuck (or a power drill if you are very careful) and glasspaper held against each side in turn. They can, of course, be sanded by hand. Cement a stub of aluminium or brass tube in the centre hole and check the alignment. Quite serviceable and attractive wheels can be made in this way.

One other form of undercarriage may be seen, bent from sheet duralumin or similar alloy and either bolted to a ply platform on the bottom of the fuselage or held in place by strong rubber bands. Axles on such undercarriages are high-quality hardened steel machine screws.

CHAPTER FIVE

Covering and finishing

Covering seems to come naturally to some but to others it's a chore. The majority of free-flight models are tissue covered and most R/C models seem to use iron-on plastic film, the remainder employing nylon or, to a decreasing degree on the grounds of cost, silk. Open-frame control-line models are probably equally divided among the three material groups but solid sheet wings and planked fuselages etc. tend towards tissue. The reasons for tissue-covering sheet balsa are primarily to achieve a good finish without a vast increase in weight and to toughen the surface against dents and scores. It also helps to seal against fuel absorption.

Tissues are available in a range of choices and references may be seen to Jap, condenser, hard, Modelspan and rag-type. Condenser tissue is creamy, semi-transparent and has a satin shine; it is used only on very lightweight indoor models and is only available from specialist suppliers. Jap is a classic lightweight tissue, in almost any colour, from Japan. Again only available from specialist suppliers, it can be distinguished by the fact that it has a grain – it will tear along the grain but not easily across it. It will also tend to shrink more across the grain. Rag tissues are fairly heavy agglomerations of random fibres, will shrink in all directions but absorb a lot of dope, i.e. they can be heavy but they are also strong. You may encounter these at a model shop. Hard tissue is light in weight, available in many colours, rustles when handled, has no grain, shrinks reasonably well in all directions but unfortunately does not possess great strength and quite often fades within a few months. However, it is widely available and used on small/light models. Modelspan is available in lightweight or heavyweight grades, usually only in white but occasionally a batch of colours comes through. This is probably the easiest lighter tissue to use, shrinking well in all directions and providing reasonable strength. The lightweight is heavier than Jap or hard and takes more dope to fill the pores so it is not ideal for smaller models, while the heavyweight should only be used for power models and large gliders.

Adhesives for tissues are very much a case of what suits you best. Many of the best builders clear dope the contacting surfaces of the balsa airframe, giving several coats until the wood grain is fairly well filled. A panel of tissue is laid in place and cellulose thinners brushed over the previously doped areas, through the tissue. The thinners etc. is allowed to dry and the panel trimmed and the edges doped down. When dry the component is lightly sprayed with water and pinned (with weights or angled-over pins) to the building board to dry and shrink. Clear dope is then applied to airproof the tissue. Alternatively you can thin balsa cement with acetone and paint this on the wood, then paint through the tissue with neat acetone.

It is possible to buy tissue cement in tubes which is spread directly on the frame. Tissue paste is also available – this must be spread on the frame and then rubbed over with a finger since any small blob will make the tissue soggy and therefore difficult to handle. The same applies to thick wallpaper paste and, to a lesser extent, white photopastes such as Gripfix or to water-thinned white PVA glue, both of which are quite widely used. Adhesive is only applied to the outside edge of the area being covered unless there is concavity, as in the case of undercambered ribs, when adhesive has to be applied to each concave member.

The usual procedure is to cut as large a panel as possible, allowing an inch or so extra all round for handling. A slabsider fuselage up to 30in. (760mm) long can be covered in four panels, a conventional wing with centre-section probably in eight — the undersides of each wing panel and centre-section (3), the upper surfaces of the wings and centre-section plus two separate tip panels (5). Always cover the undersides of the wings first, especially if there is undercamber. Tissue has a very limited ability to cover two-way curves without wrinkling so it may be necessary to cover a streamlined stringered fuselage, or a turtle-deck, in strips rather than try to do it in large panels. A circular fuselage with twelve stringers will need twelve strips of tissue, although sometimes it can be done with six, depending on the type of tissue and the curve of the fuselage.

Taking a wing underside as an example, cut the panel (grain along the span if there is a grain) and apply the adhesive along the l.e. and t.e., root rib and tip, i.e. around the outline. Lay the tissue lightly in place and press to the centre of the root rib (brush thinners at this point if using the dope method). Gently extend the tissue to the centre of the tip and press lightly onto the adhesive. Now spread the centre of the tissue panel to the l.e. and t.e. and press to tack down, then work the thumbs along the edges, gently smoothing the tissue down and putting a little tension on it at an angle. It is not necessary to try to stretch it taut, just apply it evenly and smoothly, making sure that is stuck. Reverse the wing and work back towards the root rib in the same way. Make sure all the edges are stuck before trimming surplus tissue away, but when trimming (a double-edged razor blade is again useful) leave enough overhang to paste down and round so that the top tissue will meet it and overlap it fractionally.

Should the wing have undercamber the procedure is similar but curve the tissue panel in your fingers as you first place it so

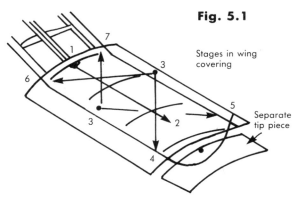

Fig. 5.1

Stages in wing covering

Separate tip piece

that it drops onto the ribs first. Follow the aforementioned procedure but pay attention to each rib and do not tension the tissue enough to lift it off the undercamber. Make sure it is firmly attached. You could also run a little dope along each rib so that subsequent water spraying will not get through to the adhesive. If it should come unstuck on shrinking after the top is covered restoring it is a messy business. You can try making a line of pinholes through the tissue along the rib centre line and rubbing cement through, pinning the tissue to the rib while it dries but a better alternative would be to cut out a two-bay panel and patch in new tissue.

For square fuselages you can either cover both sides, then bottom and top or alternatively bottom, sides then top. If the tissue is too short cover with the longer panel first, finishing on a cross-member, then add the second portion, overlapping only slightly on the cross-member. Sheet areas should be clear doped, tissue laid over the wet dope and a further coat applied. If you try to stick it around the edge, water-shrinking then doping can still leave wrinkles as the tissue expands slightly with the wet dope and the dope soaks through and sticks in some places but not others. This applies in the main to larger areas such as sheeting on wing leading edges, sheeted fuselages etc. rather than sheet panels let in at the fuselage nose.

Once covering is completed the tissue should be damped by lightly water spraying

A selection of rubber models and one glider using bright-coloured tissue finishes and no colour dope. Foreground model is a competition design using a single-blade folding propeller.

(or steaming) and left to dry out. Wings and tail should be weighted or pinned down and it may pay to cover the building board smoothly with greaseproof paper, kitchen film or thin polythene sheet (perhaps an ex-dry cleaner's bag?) so that the tissue does not stick, either from the water or, later, when doped. After drying some little local wrinkles may be evident and it is worth wetting these in case they are the result of previous uneven damping.

Most reputable model shops offer clear shrinking dope or clear non-shrinking. The former will help to reduce some wrinkles but too powerful a shrink will tend to distort any but really stiff, strong structures. It can be 'plasticised' by adding a few drops of castor oil and stirring well, a process which does not destroy its shrinking ability but which adds a degree of elasticity so that it will stop shrinking when sufficient resistance is met. Both types of clear dope fulfil the most important function which is to fill the pores in the tissue and render it airproof. Obviously close-woven tissue will require less dope to do this and the end result will be lighter. Do not use large areas of colour dope as it is very heavy. Model enamels are, surprisingly, much lighter, or car spray cans can be used to dust on the colour. If a model is tissue covered one aim must be

to keep it light and plastering it with colour defeats this object. Use coloured tissue or, if you want a particular shade, mix a little fabric dye in the water to be used for spraying on to water-shrink. If no spray is available it can be smoothed on gently with a wad of cotton wool.

Banana oil is a form of cellulose lacquer which has no shrinking effect but it will airproof and, to some extent, waterproof tissue. It resembles a thin clear varnish and is a little heavier than dope but it does not blush as easily. Blushing occurs when dope is applied in cold, damp conditions or when the tissue is not fully dry to start with and shows as white opaque patches all over the doped area. It will disappear if swabbed gently with cellulose thinners or when a further coat is applied in drier conditions.

Some experts dampen their panels of tissue before applying them, usually when using the doping method of adhesion. The blushing is extensive, but disappears when thinners or dope is applied. Even more blushing occurs when using a recent new technique of covering the panel with very thin mylar film (using adhesive from the film supplier), heat-shrinking, then coating with clear dope onto which is laid wet tissue. The blushing disappears when painted with thinners or dope. The idea behind this method is that the tissue becomes puncture proof and the whole model is stronger for an infinitesimal increase in weight.

Wet application is usually recommended for silk or nylon covering, the cloth being soaked in water, allowed to drip, then blotted in between sheets of newspaper and pinned in place while adhesive is applied. The frame-doping method, cement rubbed on with the finger and acetone painted through the cloth, or 'straight' PVA can all be used. In fact most of the adhesives mentioned can be used bearing in mind that there would be no point in using silk or, especially, nylon on an insubstantial frame so it is quite feasible to use dress-makers' pins to hold the cloth in place, giving plenty of working time. Should it dry out, the material can always be lightly sprayed with water during attachment.

Nylon in particular is likely to need several coats of dope to fill the pores but it doesn't really shrink much from the dry state. It tends to expand with water which is why it is applied wet, but water will not shrink it. The more open the weave the more likely it is that clear dope will tauten it, since shrinkage relies on the dope itself contract-ing between the fibres and the fibres them-selves are not physically affected. Unfor-tunately fillers in the dope cause cracks to appear in the finish after a few weeks, so it is necessary to keep applying plain dope until it is seen that the pores are filled. The result is extremely strong and the standard joke of having a nylon bag full of balsa bits following a bad crash has its basis in fact.

Film coverings are available in a wide variety from those resembling tissue cover-ing to heavyweight types suitable for the largest models. Some have an adhesive backing which will stick directly to bare wood on the application of heat, others need the framework outlined with a special fluid which dries into the surface and bonds with the film backing, again on the applic-ation of heat. A domestic iron provides the necessary heat source, although specially-made irons are available and are worth buying if a lot of film-covered models are to be made.

The basic method is first to paint all areas of the frame to which the film is to be applied with the preparation sold by the film sup-plier, if he recommends this for the film you have chosen. Panels are then cut, as for tissue, and the centre of one end tacked in place by touching lightly with the nose of the iron. The film is then eased evenly over the area, tacking in places, and ironed along all edges etc. The surplus is then trimmed away and the trimmed edges stuck down. The iron is now passed over the surface, not quite in contact, and the heat will cause the film to shrink. Too cool an iron will fail to ensure film adherence, too hot an iron can melt the film, so experiment first with pieces of film that have been discarded when cutting out the required panels. Some films shrink considerably and can be stuck round curved parts without wrinkles with just a little care and some practice, but these films do not normally add a great deal of torsional stiffness or strength to the structure. On the other hand, those that do are often a little harder to persuade round compound curves. The manufacturer usually supplies helpful leaflets with the film.

Decoration on film-covered models is usually carried out with further film applied over the basic colour or by specially pro-duced paints, depending on the type of film. Different films also react differently to glow or diesel fuel so there are also special fuel-proofing varnishes available. A good model shop should be able to advise you on choice of film and the necessary ancillary items. It probably sounds more complex and expensive than it actually is — remember that once the film is in place there is no outlay on dopes etc. except possibly, for a power model, fuel-proofer which would be needed whatever covering is used.

Fuel-proofer is applied to prevent oil soakage into the structure and to prevent some components of the fuel, either raw or in exhaust residue, from attacking a doped or painted finish. Commercial proofers are available but a reasonable degree of pro-tection from diesel fuel can be obtained with one-pot thin polyurethane varnish and, from glow fuel, two-pot polyurethane varnish. These are used only in the vicinity of the engine as they are fairly heavy. Film coverings should use the proofer developed and recommended by the manufacturer.

FINISH

A good finish must be, to some extent, a matter of natural ability, since two experienced modellers can use the same materials and techniques but produce widely different results. However, with practice and patience a good, pleasing finish can be obtained. Care in assembly and thorough sanding have already been stressed, and the application of tissue etc. by the doping methods, preferred by most expert modellers, has been outlined. Filling wood grain with sanding sealer is another requirement notably in sheeted areas. The sealer can be bought, or talcum powder can be added to clear non-shrinking dope. It is applied freely with a brush, allowed to dry, then fine glasspaper is used to sand virtually all of it away, leaving the grain filled and the balsa surface smooth and slightly hardened against nicks. It is still best to cover it with tissue rather than try to colour the area with dope or enamel.

Clear dopes have been dealt with and mention made of using model enamels in preference to colour dope from the weight aspect. It should be mentioned that while enamels can be applied over a doped (cellulose) surface, cellulose finishes cannot be used over enamel. Should there be any polystyrene mouldings (some kits have vacuum-formed cowlings etc.) these can be painted with enamels but not with cellulose unless a special 'dry dusting' spraying technique is used. Colour finishes should always be used sparingly because the pigments are quite heavy; only a very thin coat, sufficient to provide a non-patchy colour, should be used and if it does not dry to a gloss, so much the better. If you look at any full-size aircraft in normal light at a distance of 50m or so you will see it does not appear glittery.

Models recommended for beginners should remain tissue-coloured and clear doped. Felt pens can be used to add a little colour with negligible weight, but may not take on doped surfaces depending on the solvent used in the colour. Small areas of coloured tissue can be doped on to provide a decor, cutting out the shape(s) with a new blade and attaching by lightly wetting the area to be covered with non-shrink dope, pressing the tissue shape lightly in place then doping over the shape once wrinkles etc. have been worked out. Using transfers (decals) is not recommended on small models or on unsupported tissue surfaces, at least until you have gained some practical experience. A light, plain-looking model which flies well is infinitely preferable to a coloured and decorated heavyweight which staggers into the air and breaks because of its weight on landing!

CHAPTER SIX

Trimming and flying

An aircraft provides lift when moved through the air because the distance over the top of the wing is further than the distance underneath. Therefore, in order to avoid a hole behind the wing, the air across the top has to move faster and this reduces the pressure on the top of the wing. For a more technical explanation look up Bernoulli's Law. All the lift generated by a wing acts through one point, the *Centre of Lift*, just as all the weight of the aircraft acts through the *Centre of Gravity*, the point at which you would tie a string to hang the model exactly balanced. Then there is the force driving the plane forward, *Thrust*, and the force trying to hold it back, *Drag*. One aim of trimming is to balance the four forces — lift, weight, thrust and drag — acting on a model.

The second aim, and the first to be tackled, is glide trim since any model flying free is a glider once its power runs out. In a glide the model is always moving downward although if it is in air rising faster than the model is descending, from the ground level it is going up. While Lift and Drag are still present, Thrust has been replaced by the forward horizontal component of force generated by weight influenced by the aerodynamics of the model; weight would normally have a vertical component only but the shape of the model modifies its motion. So we must first establish the best

glide condition and, when thrust is added (engine, rubber or towline) arrange a stable set-up without disturbing the glide trim.

Provided a model balances where indicated by the designer, glide trim is not difficult to achieve. If built accurately the wing and tail incidence angles should be correct so, if balance is as specified, a hand glide should be safe. Nevertheless, the classic test glide into long grass should be followed, if possible, as initially the speed required may not be judged too well — too slow a launch will lead to an immediate stall, too fast will produce a swoop usually followed by a stall. A stall occurs when the airflow over the wing breaks down, usually because of loss of speed, the model dropping out of the air. However, a too rapid change of attitude can cause the airflow to break away at any speed, leading to a high-speed stall and, most probably, a flick half-roll and dive. Long grass cushions the arrival of the model and goes some way towards reducing damage in the event of a mishap.

If launched slightly nose-down, pointing at a spot on the ground around 50ft. (15m) ahead, and at about the right speed, the model may climb, the nose drop and a dive ensue, followed by climb, nose drop, dive and so on. This is stalling flight and the cures are (a) increase the weight in the nose; (b) decrease the wing incidence by

Fig. 6.1

Smooth glide · Stall · Dive

packing balsa strip(s) under the trailing edge; (c) increase the tailplane incidence by packing under the leading edge or (d) move the whole wing back if the design permits this. *Only ever alter one thing at a time* and only by a small amount at a time. If the model glides very steeply or dives, the reverse steps apply — (a) reduce the weight at the nose or add weight to the tail; (b) increase the wing incidence; (c) decrease the tail incidence or (d) move the wing forward. In the case of a stall where the wing cannot be moved, beware of reducing the angular difference between the wing and the tail too much; safe trim is when the wing is always at a slightly greater (positive) angle of incidence to that of the tailplane, so in this instance nose ballast may be the only feasible adjustment.

Having reached a reasonable gliding angle, try if possible a longer glide, down a sloping field or from a hillock, which will give the model a little longer to settle. If not, wait until short flights are made but first establish whether the model is turning one way or the other. This can be caused by warps or misalignment of the surfaces and the effect may be heightened with increase in speed under power, so it is desirable to find out what is causing the turn and remedy or counteract it. There is little else to be done in the case of a towline

glider except a little fine tuning to produce large circles in flight while maintaining a straight tow and perhaps tiny changes in nose ballast to achieve a floating glide without undulations. Tow it gently initially and watch carefully what happens on release; it goes without saying that test flights for trimming should not take place in a stiff breeze. The usual hook position on a glider is on a line passing through the centre of gravity at an angle of 60 degrees to the horizontal.

With rubber or engine-powered models a further dimension is added once a satisfactory glide has been achieved — the power thrust line — which modifies the forces already balanced in the glide. Since any successful flight will require the model to glide, the trim already found should not be altered, except possibly by small rudder adjustments. Any change in the glide trim produced by the power line of thrust should be cancelled only by the changes in that thrust line. This is not as difficult as it may seem although with a high-powered model there is always a slight risk, even when full power is worked up to slowly.

If you wound a rubber model then held the prop and let go of the rest, you would not be surprised if the whole model rotated. Air resistance does not hold the propeller still but it does have a braking effect on it and this effect is passed to the model, giving it a tendency to rotate in the opposite direction to the propeller. This is called *torque* effect and it results in the model turning to the left. This applies to a right-handed prop (turns anti-clockwise when viewed from the front) as well as engine-powered models. Left-handed props are normally seen only on twin-engined or pusher type models. With a powerful motor the torque effect may well cause the model to turn and dive into the ground on the left. One obvious cure is to apply right rudder, but this will

A nice launch by a young lady — note the follow-through of the hand. The model is already climbing and torque effect is banking it left.

make the glide circles different, possibly even tight enough for the model to spiral rapidly down when the power runs out. However, if the line of thrust is altered by pointing the propeller shaft a degree or two to the right, a sideways component of thrust is introduced which will turn the model to the right, thus offsetting torque effect to a greater or lesser degree. This alteration is called *sidethrust* and is made on a rubber model by packing the port side of the noseblock or on a power model by using bolts smaller than their holes, slackening the nuts and twisting the engine, then re-tightening. The amount has to be a matter of experiment.

The other effect of the thrust line relates to its position in respect of the centre of drag, which is of course fixed. If the thrust line passes above it, it will produce a nose-down couple, and if below it, a nose-up couple. Due to the drag generated by the wing and its usual position in an aero-dynamic sense, it is rare for the thrust line to be higher than the centre of drag, so in most cases motor power tends to create a nose-up tendency. The answer here is to tilt the propeller shaft downward, called *down-thrust*, again by packing the noseblock or, with an engine, placing thin washers under the lugs at the rear mounting holes. With high-powered models having a tendency to loop, a little extra sidethrust, rather than downthrust, will turn the incipient loop into a spiral climb, but this is entering the realms of expert techniques. With a beginner's model, if it tends to stall under power, or fly as if it was going 'up stairs', it is safer to put in a little downthrust.

When a model turns, the outside wing travels fractionally faster and therefore generates more lift than the inside wing, causing the model to bank. Increasing turn can cause the inside wing to stall, increas-ing bank leads to sideslipping inwards, when the weathercock action of the fin turns the nose down and the model spiral dives into the ground. This is one reason for aiming for wide circles! Dihedral angle —

the V of the wings — helps in that on bank-ing the lower wing is presented to the airstream at a more advantageous angle for its total span while the raised wing has a lower angle of attack over its span, or over a foreshortened span if the design incorporates sweepback, thus producing a force which tends to roll the model out of its bank. If you have made the chuck glider in Chapter 3 you can hold it pointing towards you in a bank and see the difference in the wings. Another trimming aid is wash-out — reduced incidence angle — at each wingtip. Reducing the angle allows the inside wing to remain lifting longer by delaying the stall, while the faster-moving outer wing will suffer increased drag, tending to help reduce the turn, and may quite possibly experience a touch of up-aileron effect opposing the bank. Wash-out can be built in by propping the trailing edges at both wingtips while weighting the leading edges down during the period when the covering is shrinking. Only a small amount is needed, say ⅛in. (3mm) on a 36in. (900mm) wing.

Warps can often be taken out of flying surfaces by warming them in front of an electric fire (with care) and pinning them down, or holding twisted the opposite way until cool, or even by re-doping. In the same way, wash-out can be induced into a panel. However, leaving a model exposed to hot sunshine can undo all your mini-strations by altering tensions in the covering. Some keen competitors mature their models for some months before fully trimming them, in order to ensure consistency.

Air is funny stuff — you can have dead air, or poor air in which a model glides down quickly, good air where it glides well, buoyant air where it glides exceptionally well, rising air or lift and corresponding descending air or sink. It doesn't get heated by the sun but by conduction from contact with surfaces which are heated by the sun and it is this which sets up convection, with rising and correspondingly sinking air currents. The difference between the heat absorbed and reflected into the air by, for

example, a factory building and a grass field, or a cornfield and a wood or lake is considerable, giving rise to warmed bubbles of air which break away and rise in a continual stream. These are generally called *thermals* and they can be very strong, accelerating as they rise and travelling downwind at wind speed, taking with them any models which have flown into them and remain circling within them.

As models became more efficient and a greater number were lost, a means was sought of ending the flight without damaging the model. The eventual answer proved to be a simple arrangement of rubber bands which, when activated, released the tailplane to pop up to a negative angle of about 30 degrees, completely stalling the wing and causing the model to descend vertically in a horizontal attitude. The release was (and is) usually by a length of smouldering lamp wick which melts the key retaining band when it burns down to it. The arrangement, called a *dethermaliser* or DT, can also be triggered by a clockwork timer mechanism for a small weight penalty. It is a refinement which the beginner probably need not worry about at first, but nevertheless a name and address should always be marked on every model.

GLIDER TOWING

Ideally an assistant is needed and a winch is helpful. The assistant holds the model pointing into the wind, slightly nose-up, and hooks on the towline ring. The flier holds the line to hang in a slight loop which will hang vertical when he is directly into wind. He then moves to take up the slack, signals and walks or trots into the wind. As the pull comes on the model the assistant, moving forward with the flier, eases his grip to allow the model to rise out of his hand. In calm, the flier will probably have to run to start the model climbing, in a brisk breeze he may stand still or even run towards his assistant to reduce the model's speed. If it should start to veer, a gentle pull in the opposite direction is required immediately, but if it veers sharply the line should be slackened to release the ring from the hook, even to the extent of throwing the winch towards the model! A light pennant about 6in. (150mm) square near the ring will help to blow it off the hook. With a straight tow, slow up and allow the model to settle at the top of the climb before releasing all tension. The winch can be a drum on a hand-drill, or made from Meccano or from a hand-grinding device made to clamp on a bench; these used to be sold in chain stores and come up surprisingly often at car boot sales or on used tool market stalls. Commercial winches are available from specialist suppliers.

RUBBER WINDING

The specified (or appropriate) length of rubber should be tied into a loop with a reef knot and an assistant should stretch the knot and ends while half a dozen turns of knitting wool are tied tightly, close against the knot each side. Hook the loop on a doorknob and measure off to make the requisite number of strands. Secure the ends by looping rubber bands tightly round. Wash the rubber to remove any dust or chalk residue, dry carefully with a clean soft cloth and lubricate with purpose-made rubber lubricant (specialist suppliers), silicone lubricant (for car fanbelts etc.) or castor oil. Do not allow it to come into contact with dirt or dust and keep it from light by storing in a clean tin in a cool place.

To braid a motor, undo one end of the skein and halve the strands approximately, marking the centre with a wisp of wool. Wind on about 50 turns, grasp the centre and realign the ends. On release, the motor will coil itself to a shorter length. Adjust turns until the final length is the distance between the hooks in the model. To wind, fix a wire hook securely in a hand-drill and engage it in the loop formed on the propshaft. If no loop, protect the wire with rubber sleeving from discarded electrical flex, cycle valve rubber etc. and hook directly to the motor, having removed the prop assembly which has to be replaced on the wound motor. An assistant holds the model, ideally with a finger and thumb ahead of and touching the dowel, and the other hand holding the nose; two fingers should cross the nose aperture and the motor passes between these fingers so that it is not chafed.

A rubber motor should be broken in by first winding 100 turns, next time 200, then 350, resting for at least a few minutes between winds. It should be stretched while winding, at least three times its unwound length, winding on turns as it is stretched out, then winding back in until it is close to the fuselage nose on the final turns. Stretch-winding allows more energy to be stored in the rubber so that more power is delivered for longer.

Modern practice in many instances is to use a 'stooge' for winding. This is a frame, securely fastened to the ground, capable of positioning and supporting the model, which is retained in place by a stout wire passing between two strong lugs and through an aluminium tube on the model used in place of the rear motor dowel. This

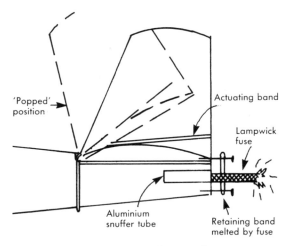

Fig. 6.2 – Dethermaliser

allows single-handed winding. Some fliers remove the noseblock and pass a 'blast tube' down the fuselage, surrounding the motor so that if it breaks it will not destroy the fuselage. Another method is to wind outside the fuselage and use a rod to pass the wound motor into the fuselage, but these methods are really only used by keen competitors anxious to wind their models to the limit for each flight.

POWER MODELS

There is a knack to starting most model engines and this should be practised thoroughly on a test bench before installing the motor and rushing off to the flying field. If in difficulty seek help from an experienced modeller, though little trouble should be encountered if the manufacturer's instructions are followed and fresh fuel used. For initial flights the motor can be run rich, which slows it down, and/or the propeller can be fitted back to front, which reduces its efficiency, thus allowing the chance to trim the model without going off at full bore. Running rich simply means opening the fuel needle-valve, which will allow a two-stroke engine to four-stroke, a difference which can easily be heard. The more running-in an engine has the easier it

RUBBER MOTORS

Rubber varies considerably, even from batch to batch of the same type, so that unless a motor is made up and tested to destruction it is impossible to be certain of how many turns it will take or how much torque it will deliver. These figures can only be used as a rough guide!

TURNS PER INCH FOR A LUBRICATED, RUN-IN MOTOR NUMBER OF STRANDS										APPROX WEIGHT OF RUBBER	
										YARDS PER POUND	FEET PER OUNCE
SIZE INCHES	8	10	12	14	16	18	20	22	24	75	14
¼ x ½₄	30	26	24	22	20	–	–	–	–	96	18
¼ x /₃₀	33	30	28	26	25	24	–	–	–	100	19
³/₁₆ x ½₄	35	32	29	27	26	24	23	21	–	130	24
³/₁₆ x ⅟₃₀	37	34	31	29	28	27	26	25	24	135	25
⅛ x ½₄	44	40	36	33	31	30	29	28	26		

These pictures show virtually the same engine design except that that on the left uses a glowplug and that on the right is a diesel — note the difference in the cylinder heads. The glow engine also has a simple cylindrical silencer rather than a 'straight-through' exhaust.

will be to start and control.

It is important to use the right fuel — ask at a model shop if you do not have the manufacturer's instructions. Many small glow engines will not run on 'straight' fuel but need a percentage of nitro-methane added to the basic methanol/castor mix. This fuel is not suitable for diesels, which need a paraffin/castor/ether mix. Stale fuel makes starting very difficult, especially with a diesel, as does a discharged battery in the case of glow motors.

A glow engine has only a needle-valve control, so if the plug is glowing and fuel is getting through, it must fire. Occasional pops as the prop is flicked probably means too little fuel, while too much fuel may pro-

A vintage '60' 10 cc petrol (spark ignition) engine installed in an 8 ft. (2.5 m) free flight model. Lever behind propeller is ignition advance/retard. Runs on petrol/oil mixture and tiny tank visible would give perhaps two-minute run!

duce a sizzling sound and a flooded engine. Diesels have the advantage that they do not need a heavy starter battery, lead and glowplug clip, but on the other hand they have two variable controls — the needle-valve and compression adjustment — so a little experience is needed to be able to recognise which control needs to be moved to get the engine running well. The quickest way to establish settings is to choke the engine (turning the prop with a finger over the air intake) and flick the prop until resistance is felt as excess fuel is transferred to the cylinder, then back off compression and flick, gradually increasing compression until it fires. It will then either flood (close needle a little) or require choking again (open needle a little). You will soon acquire the knack of flicking the propeller hard and fast and getting the controls correctly set.

CHAPTER SEVEN

Thumbelina

This little model can be built as either a towline glider or with rubber power or even, if you wish, as convertible between the two. It is intended that the pages should be photocopied to provide a plan, alternatively a tracing could be made. Note that it is all straight lines, apart from the upper line of the wing section and the corners of the flying surfaces which have a tiny curve sanded in. Apart from a black tissue (or felt pen) cabin, all the decoration is also straight lines but the model still manages to look attractive (see the cover of this book). The only other curves arise if you make the rubber-powered model and make a propeller, the blades of which have curved outlines. Alternatively you could buy a plastic prop from a model shop.

The materials required are very simple, mostly $\frac{1}{16}$in. sheet and $\frac{1}{16}$in. square. You will need two $\frac{1}{16} \times 3 \times 36$in. sheets of softish balsa ($1\frac{1}{2} \times 75 \times 900$mm). It should be light but firm, soft enough to mark quite deeply with a thumbnail. For the fuselage fillets three quite soft $\frac{1}{16}$in. square are required and for the wing spars three lengths of fairly hard $\frac{1}{16}$ sq. (or two $\frac{1}{16}$ and one $\frac{1}{16} \times \frac{1}{8}$in.) plus a length of $\frac{3}{16}$in. sq. and one of $\frac{1}{8} \times \frac{1}{4}$in., both medium to soft. Other odds and ends may be found in the house e.g. a bamboo skewer (for kebabs) about $\frac{3}{32}$in. (2mm) diameter, a paper clip and a scrap of acetate sheet for reinforcement areas. It

would be helpful if you could obtain a scrap of $\frac{1}{4}$in. (6mm) balsa or a small block, but there are ways round this.

The best way to build is to photocopy the pages of drawings and cut the three parts of the fuselage, sticking them accurately together. Don't cut them to the outline but just separate areas of paper. Trim off one A-A and one B-B and overlay the pieces accurately — the straight lines top and bottom should make line-up easy. Use a glue stick or adhesive tape to secure them. All three wing panels are the same in plan. so you can either build three times over one copy or make three copies.

First draw the fuselage side on one balsa sheet, following the centre of the three lines round the outline. (The outside line shows the top and bottom sheeting, the inside dashed line the $\frac{1}{16}$in. square fillets.) Cut out using a steel rule or similar metal straight edge, then lay the piece over the remainder of the sheet and cut round, again with the rule, to obtain the second side. Lay the sides flat, ensuring one left and one right, and pin and cement the $\frac{1}{16}$in. square round the edges. Note that there is no fillet right at the tail end. Leave to dry. While you are waiting you can cut out the fin, tailplane and 13 wing ribs.

At this point it is desirable to decide whether the model is to be glider only, rubber only or convertible. The differences are only slight but it is best to be clear from

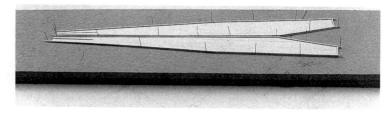

The fuselage sides laid on the building board with the fillet strips cemented and temporarily pinned.

Simple structure still requires care to get everything square and true.

the outset. First, the wing spars. The three spars can be $\frac{1}{16}$in. square for the rubber model but if either of the other versions is chosen use $\frac{1}{16} \times \frac{1}{8}$in. for the centre one of the three, which means cutting those notches deeper. If glider-only, cut two $\frac{3}{4}$in. wide strips of $\frac{1}{16}$in. sheet and cement to the fuselage sides inside the nose ends, then cut a former, G1, from $\frac{1}{16}$in. and when assembling the sides together fit across the fuselage as shown. This forms a box when the top and bottom sheeting is added. Drill a hole in the top and drop in slivers of lead, or lead shot, to balance. Cover the hole with tape for tests and cement a plug in when satisfied. A noseblock as shown would look attractive but to save buying a block, or a pack of balsa offcuts, one can be laminated from spare $\frac{1}{16}$in. sheet and cemented to the nose. The towhook can be bent from a straightened paper clip, cemented in place then, when dry, reinforced by a postage-stamp size piece of nylon tights cemented over the flat area.

If built as a convertible, follow rubber construction (except for the change of wing spar and addition of towhook) but there will have to be an alternative noseblock with a box firmly built onto its back or a

screw or bolt fitted through and solder strip wound round as necessary for nose weight. If a further length of bamboo is cemented through the bottom of the fuselage sides, about 2in. back from the nose, a rubber band can be stretched from one side, round the noseblock and back to the other end of the bamboo. A small groove cut or filed across the noseblock will locate the band and the block will be held firmly in place.

Now, back to cutting the wing ribs. Trace the rib shape on to a piece of thick card or thin ply and cut out. You can use this as a template either to draw round 13 times or actually to guide the blade to cut out the ribs. Assemble the ribs into a stack, aligning the flat bottoms and leading edges, and push two pins through. Lightly sand so that

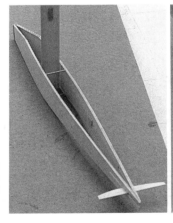

Assembling the fuselage sides using, in this case, a plastic ruler to hold things square. Nose is rubber-banded and scrap piece checks alignment of tail slots. Far picture, first piece of underside sheeting and nose reinforcement strips.

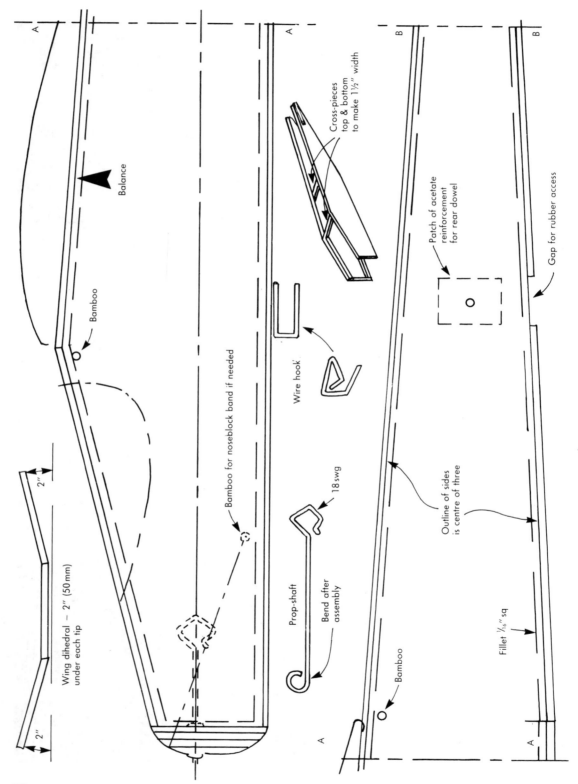

Balance

Bamboo

Cross-pieces top & bottom to make 1½" width

Wire hook

18 swg

Prop-shaft

Bend after assembly

Bamboo for noseblock band if needed

Wing dihedral – 2" (50 mm) under each tip

2"

2"

Patch of acetate reinforcement for rear dowel

Gap for rubber access

Outline of sides is centre of three

Bamboo

Fillet ⅟₁₆" sq

50

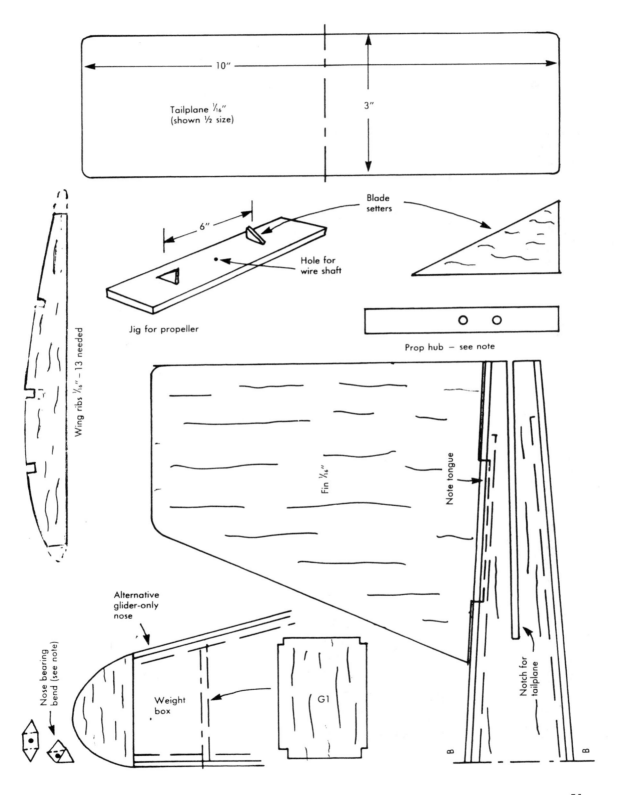

10"

3"

Tailplane ¹⁄₁₆"
(shown ½ size)

Blade setters

Wing ribs ¹⁄₁₆" – 13 needed

6"

Hole for wire shaft

Jig for propeller

Prop hub – see note

Fin ¹⁄₁₆"

Note tongue

Alternative glider-only nose

Nose bearing bend (see note)

Weight box

G1

Notch for tailplane

B

B

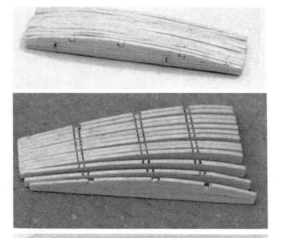

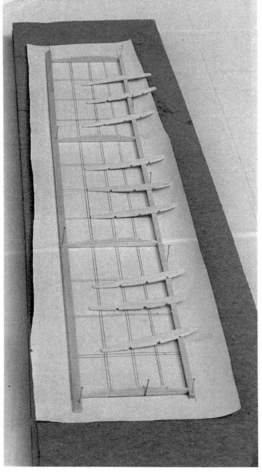

all the ribs are smooth and the same size, then mark the notches for the spars across the stack and cut out. To make things easier, the wing has been designed so that if you draw (or photocopy) the three panels as one piece, the l.e. and t.e. can be pinned down and the ribs cemented in with everything flat. The centre panel spars are then added and small V cuts made in the l.e. and t.e. at the dihedral breaks. Crack the bottoms of the V cuts, squeeze in cement and lift each tip 2 in. (50mm), blocking in place with books or parallel pieces of wood. Fit the outer panel spars, leave to dry, then add gussets and re-cement the spar joints at the dihedral breaks. When dry, carefully sand the l.e. and t.e. to the sections shown and lightly round off the tips.

The fuselage is 1½in. (38mm) wide beneath the wing l.e. and t.e., which means a 1¼in. gap allowing for ¹⁄₁₆in. sides and ¹⁄₁₆in. fillets. If you can find a block or box 1¼in. wide, or two small cans or bottles 1¼in. diameter, the sides can be propped against it (or them) while four cross-pieces (or spacers) are inserted at the l.e. and t.e. positions. When dry the tail ends can be drawn together and cemented and the nose ends drawn in and ¾in. spacers cemented in to make the nose 1in. wide overall. An alternative is to cut rectangles from cereal-packet card and assemble the sides using these to hold things square; they can be slightly bent and removed once the top or bottom of the fuselage has been sheeted.

Sight along the fuselage to make sure that the sides form symmetrical curves. If one is straighter than the other, hold it for a few seconds in steam from a kettle spout, gently easing it to symmetry then holding as it cools. Place it on the remaining ¹⁄₁₆in. sheet with the front bottom in contact and

Top, the wing ribs, as cut, pinned together for sanding, and, centre, the sanded ribs with spar notches marked. Bottom, the leading and trailing edge strips pinned down and the four hardest ribs cemented at dihedral breaks and tips.

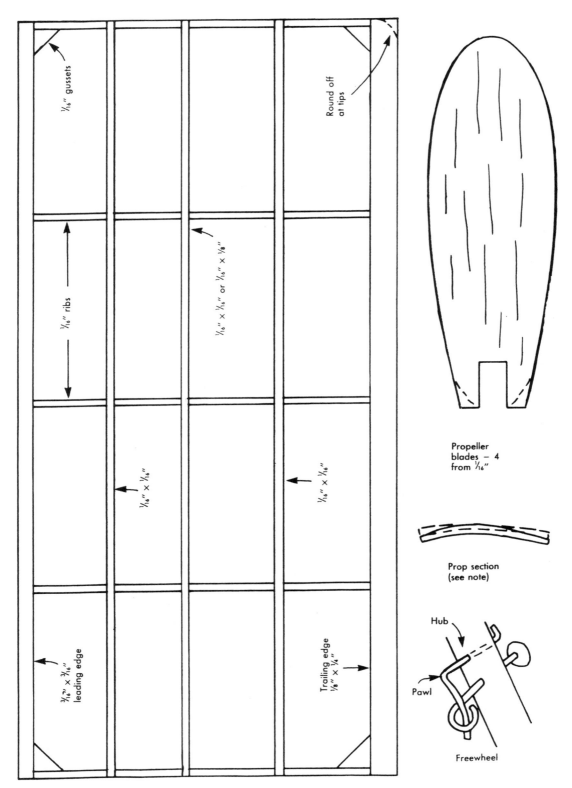

$\frac{1}{16}$" gussets

Round off at tips

$\frac{1}{16}$" ribs

$\frac{1}{16}$" × $\frac{1}{16}$" or $\frac{1}{16}$" × $\frac{1}{8}$"

$\frac{1}{16}$" × $\frac{1}{16}$"

$\frac{1}{16}$" × $\frac{1}{16}$"

$\frac{3}{16}$" × $\frac{3}{16}$" leading edge

Trailing edge $\frac{1}{8}$" × $\frac{1}{4}$"

Propeller blades — 4 from $\frac{1}{16}$"

Prop section (see note)

Hub

Pawl

Freewheel

53

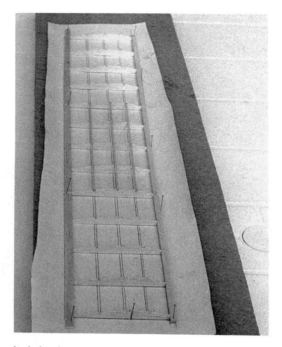

a little thicker than the bamboo used for the wing dowels, perhaps a bit of a solid garden cane or a ⅛in. (3mm) bamboo skewer. Leave a small part of the underside unsheeted under the dowel so that the rubber motor can easily be engaged.

Cut the fin and tailplane and sand the edges. Mark accurately and cut the slot in the fuselage for the fin tongue and check the tailplane slots for alignment. Cement the fin and tailplane in place and lay a ruler across the wing seat, sighting to ensure that the tailplane is exactly parallel with the ruler and that the fin is exactly at right angles to the tailplane. This is important for good flying characteristics. For harder wearing, a strip of ⅛in. or ³⁄₁₆in. wide hard balsa can be cut to form a frame at the nose, as shown in the photograph, but this is not essential and, of course, should not be included if the glider-only version with a fixed noseblock is built. The fuselage and tail surfaces will benefit from a *thin* coat of non-shrink clear dope, banana oil or sanding sealer, sanded with very fine glasspaper to a smooth finish when dry.

Cover the wing, bottom and top, with lightweight tissue, using six panels, lightly water-shrink and then give a coat of thinned dope taking precautions against warps (see Chapter 5). Add any required trim, using strips of coloured tissue doped on, or a small amount of car trim tape or a decal (transfer), but do not add too much weight.

lightly draw round the area in contact. Cut out the shape and cement and pin in place. Leave this to dry, then remove the pins. Repeat for the remainder of the top and bottom. It may be necessary to use several pieces as the available sheet balsa dwindles. Remember to cut a little outside the lines and sand the edges down to a flush fit when dry. Provision for the rear dowel for the rubber should be made by cementing acetate patches inside and drilling through for the size dowel available. This should be

Opposite, top, the wing built flat with the centre section spars in place.

Right, the leading and trailing edges cracked and cemented with the tip raised 1½in. (measured to the bottom of the tip rib) and the remaining spars added. The finished tip shows slight rounding and gussets in place.

Opposite, bottom, noseblock for the (convertible) glider version. Note notch for rubber band. Wing bands are just visible; these are crossed over wing.

The glider version of the prototype weighed a shade under 1¾oz (nearly 50gm) in flying condition.

For the glider around ½oz (14gm) of ballast will be needed, more if you used heavier balsa than the original. Add weight in the ballast box, or nuts or turns of solder to the bolt or screw if used, until the model balances on the centre spar. A finger underneath at the dihedral break each side will give a reasonable idea of balance. Try a gentle hand glide, following the procedure in Chapter 6. A piece of aluminium foil or acetate sheet can be cemented on the t.e. of the rudder, or on the t.e. of one wing near the tip and bent as needed to produce a very wide, gentle turn. For towing, a spool of thread will be adequate. Tie a small wire ring to the end and a tissue or light cloth pennant about a foot from the ring. Use only about 30ft. (10m) of line at first

and try to tow at only just above the model's flying speed — in only a light breeze you could probably stand still and the model will still climb. Your assistant should not try to launch the model, but let it fly out of his hand. Adjust the trim as necessary, then enjoy longer flights.

A plastic propeller of 8 or 9in. diameter (200–230mm) can be used for the rubber-powered version of this model, or one can be carved from a balsa block 9 × 1 × 5⁄8in. (230 × 25 × 15mm) or that shown on the model used. First cut four 1⁄16in. blades, cement together in pairs and position while the cement is wet on a jar or tin 3in. (75mm) diameter as shown, winding round with soft string or using rubber bands. Allow to dry, then sand to approximately the section shown. Cut a 2in. (50mm) length from a round pencil and check that the notches in the blades are a good fit on it. Drill a fine

The propeller blades rubber-banded to a suitable diameter bottle.

that the corner of the hook is in line with the straight part of the shaft. Cut two tiny shapes, as drawn, from a piece of thin tinplate (from a can or biscuit tin etc.) using an old pair of scissors and punch a hole in each with a sharp panel pin or fine nail; it is better to punch the holes first and then cut out. Bend the triangular tabs to 90 degrees. The noseblock, which can be laminated from $\frac{1}{16}$in. sheet (or cut from $\frac{1}{4}$in. sheet from a balsa pack) has a plug on the back made from two laminations of $\frac{1}{16}$in. which exactly fits the nose aperture and, if necessary, may be held in by a rubber band as previously described. Push a pin through on the shaft line, then follow the hole through with a piece of the 18g wire, checking that it is straight through and not pointing up or down or to one side. Slide a tinplate bearing on each side and press the tabs into the balsa, remove, cement and push back in. Cut a $\frac{3}{4}$in. piece of insulation tube from an old piece of electrical flex and slide onto the shaft, working it round the hook by lightly wetting if necessary (rubber tube is better than plastic but either can be used).

hole accurately through the centre and another $\frac{3}{8}$in. (9mm) from it. A broken needle can be used as a drill, either by snapping off the eye and using it in a hand-drill or by pushing the point into a piece of wood and heating the other end to burn a hole through. Alternatively, and the way an expert would do it, use a piece of 18swg aluminium or brass tube and drill a $\frac{1}{16}$in. hole, enlarging it as necessary with a round needle file, then roughening the outside of the tube and cementing it in the hole.

Bend the propeller shaft hook, ensuring

Slip the shaft through the bearings and slide on a pair of cup washers. If these cannot be found use tiny flat washers with a glass bead between, or in desperation just a glass bead! Slide on the prop (the

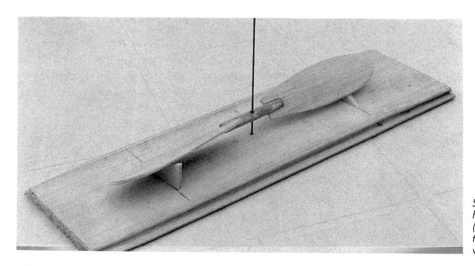

Set the blades and hub up on the the jig (see sketch) ensuring that the wire is vertical.

The glider version about to be towed up. Note tissue pennant on towline and slight nose-up angle of model.

right way round) and bend the little loop on the front end using round-nose pliers. (If a plastic prop is used it is likely to have a moulded-in ramp on the front of the hub, in which case only a right-angle bend is needed on the shaft. You then have to wind by hooking the rubber to the winder, holding the wound motor to unhook and then hook the propeller assembly in place.) The loop allows easy winding and a small pawl through the second hole in the prop hub makes an efficient freewheel device (see sketch).

All that is now needed is the rubber motor, made up as described earlier from five feet of ⅛in rubber (150 × 3mm) into four strands, braided to end up about 12in. (30mm) long. Insert in the model and balance it on the centre spar as before. It is best to leave out the bamboo dowels and slip the wing in place with one large, thin rubber band, allowing it to be slid fore and aft to find the position required for balance. This can then be marked and the dowels fitted as appropriate. It is not possible to state categorically where the model will

Launching the rubber powered version should start from this position. Launch level or slightly downward.

The simple structure of Thumbelina is clear from this view. Make sure that the tailplane and fin are square to the fuselage and line up properly with the wing.

To carve a propeller start with a medium to hard balsa black 9 × 1½ × 1 in. Mark off into quarters, then follow the first picture. Saw out and mark the ends into thirds, then draw on the sides as picture 2. Saw the end tapers, then carve the back of the blades, picture 3. Finally carve the front, cut the hub and blades to shape and balance the prop by trying it on a wire through the shaft hole, sanding the heavy blade or side until it will remain still in any position.

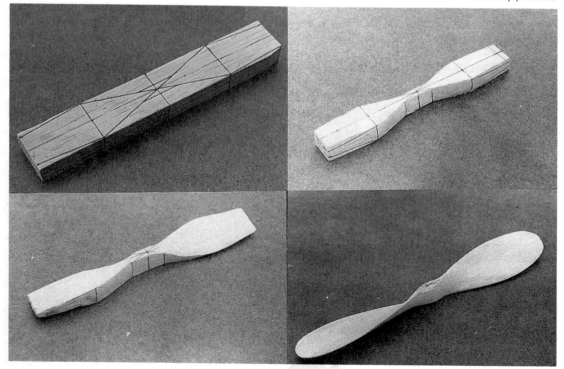

balance because of variables such as the weight of the sheet balsa used and the possible differences in weight between a plastic prop or a wood one. Small adjustments may be made by packing a $\frac{1}{16}$in. strip (or up to $\frac{1}{8}$in.) under the wing l.e. if the glide is too steep or under the t.e. if the glide tends to be stally. Try a few turns on the rubber initially and add down and/or side thrust with thin packing as needed. The motor when broken in should take at least 600 turns. For more power use either six strands of $\frac{1}{8}$in. or four of $\frac{3}{16}$in. and don't forget your name and address on the model!

CHAPTER EIGHT

Radio control

Strictly speaking, radio-controlled models hardly come under the category of basic aeromodelling, but since they attract the most publicity, and indeed some people think that they are the only form of model aircraft, some outline should be included. It should be said that the person who is prepared to spend a lot of money on a finished model or an almost-ready-to-fly (ARTF) kit and associated radio is less likely to become a committed aeromodeller than someone who wants to build and fly free-flight models in order to learn; there is a through-put of people who take up R/C flying in the easiest way possible but who next year will be dinghy sailing or off-road racing or some other pursuit which takes their fancy for a short while. Equally, of course, there are radio fliers who have been doing it since the very early days and still derive enormous pleasure from it. Many of these have turned to accurate scale modelling, but there is still a lot of enthusiasm for aerobatics and demanding areas such as helicopters and pylon racing.

Radio permits a model to do anything of which a full-size aeroplane is capable, with the difference that the pilot is on the ground, so instead of instantaneous recognition of and reaction to changing circumstances, the pilot has to wait until circumstances develop to a recognisable point before he can react. In the case of an expert, any delay is infinitesimal but a novice can experience a lot of difficulty. Orientation is a problem — to make the model turn to your left as it goes away from you, *left* rudder is applied, to make it turn to your left as it comes towards you *right* rudder is needed and some people have great difficulty getting used to this. Almost all beginners have at some

stage allowed the model to get too far away and cannot decide whether it is flying away or towards them, or even sometimes if it is the right way up! Most clubs have one or two instructors who can teach new members to fly and no-one should be too proud to take advantage of such opportunities.

A radio system is initially identified by its number of functions or channels, which may be single, 2, 3, 4, 5, 6, 7 or even 8 in number. It is advisable to look ahead and buy an outfit which will allow you more scope than you at first need. For example, a rudder-only (1f) or rudder/throttle (2f) trainer is fine, but you will progress to elevator (3f) and then to ailerons (4f), so it makes sense to buy a four-function set at the outset, using only such channels as are required to start with. Each function requires a servo, which is the electro-mechanical device which actually operates the function and simply plugs into the receiver which switches it on and off in the direction selected by the control on the transmitter. Servos are fairly expensive, so if you are going to fly rudder-only, you need only buy one initially but buy a four-function transmitter and receiver. You can add further servos as needed and some sets are extendable by the manufacturer, who can add further channels at a moderate cost.

One early decision is whether to use dry or rechargeable nickel-cadmium batteries. The cost of nicads plus a charger does add quite a bit to the initial expense but will give probably three seasons of flying without further outlay except for the negligible amount of electricity needed for charging whereas dry cells will need to be replaced after every two hours or so of use. At current prices, nicads could prove cheaper after

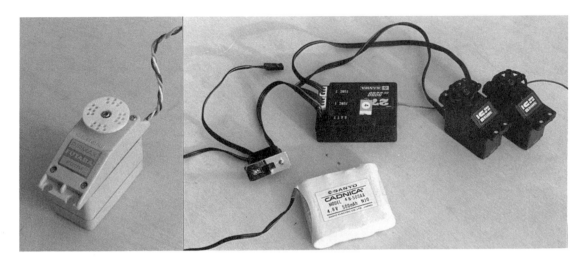

less than twenty flying sessions. However, it is possible to start by using dry cells and change to nicads at a later stage. Always read the supplier's instructions and follow them faithfully to get good results from both radio and nicads. Incidentally, a basic dry cell is 1.5 volts but a nicad is 1.2, so six of the latter give 7.2 volts as against 9.0 from dry cells. Modern radio is designed to cope with this difference.

The receiver is simply a small box with sockets for servo plugs, wires for battery input and switch and an aerial wire, plus an additional socket for a crystal. The crystal is a slice of quartz which resonates at a particular frequency that is matched by a crystal in the transmitter. These crystals control the radio frequency on which the equipment operates and they can be changed to another pair to alter the frequency, which is why a number of models can operate simultaneously. Normal procedure is to wrap the receiver in foam rubber and hold it against a bulkhead, platform or box built into the model using rubber bands. The servos are mounted in cut-outs in a ply shelf or on rails across the fuselage, the securing screws or bolts passing through rubber

Photos above show, left, a servo, one of which is needed for each control, as a rule, and, right, airborne equipment for two functions — switch and charging socket, nicad pack, receiver and two servos.

Right, attractive 51½ in. span Sopwith Dolphin for a ·45 cu. in. four-stroke engine and four radio functions by E. Sapcote.

Almost anything is possible with radio. This 68 in. A-10 Thunderbolt uses twin ducted fans instead of propellers, using two ·40 (6½ cc) two-stroke engines. Designed and built by Trevor Waters.

grommets to absorb engine vibration. As the heaviest item, the battery pack is usually stowed forward of the rest of the radio, again wrapped in rubber (not plastic) foam so that it will not damage radio components in the event of a crash.

There are three general forms of linkage from the servos to the controls — pushrods, snakes and closed loops. Pushrods, if short, are wires fitted with clevises at each end, one to engage the servo output disc or arm and the other to a horn on the control. The clevises are threaded on to a screw thread on the wire so that the pushrod overall length can be adjusted. For longer pushrods, a square hardish balsa strip or a balsa dowel is used, the clevis ends of the wire being cut off and bound to the balsa rod.

Friction-free movement is required and the control should be able to move a little farther than the servo movement so that there is no risk of stalling the servo motor.

Snakes consist of wires, bowden cables or fine plastic tubes sliding inside an outer tube, thus allowing operation through gentle bends. The inner member has a clevis on either end and the outer tube has to be secured in place at intervals so that it cannot be displaced by the movement of the inner part. Low friction is again important, also adequate movement to avoid servo stall. A common application for a snake is throttle operation, the tube passing through drilled holes in engine bulkheads etc. where a pushrod would need slots to accommodate the slight sideways movement inherent in its

Five functions — including retracting undercarriage — are used in this 10 cc powered 54 in. fast aerobatic design by Clive Weller. At well over 100 m.p.h., such designs are not for beginners!

A two-function transmitter. Left-hand stick may operate throttle or elevator, right-hand one rudder or ailerons. Meter shows state of charge of nicad batteries.

action. A closed loop operates with a pull whichever way the control is required to move, by means of a double horn on the control connected to both sides of the servo arm by two lengths of light wire or strong thread. There is therefore no danger of pushing an insufficiently stiff pushrod which could bow in the middle, preventing full control being applied.

Modern radio allows whatever degree of control application the flier wants. If the rudder stick on the transmitter is moved halfway left, the model's rudder will move halfway left and so on, the sticks being sprung so that control surfaces return to neutral when the sticks are released. The exception to this is throttle, where the stick remains in the position to which it is moved. There are trims on the transmitter which are used to bias the controls, giving about 10% of total movement. For example, if the model is not flying straight the rudder trim is used to adjust it so that there is no need to hold the stick permanently off-centre. An additional use of a trim is to put it fully to one side when, if the stick is also put hard over to that side momentarily, it can operate a switch. Move the trim nearer to the centre and the stick can be put hard over without activating the switch since it does not have the extra control movement given by the trim. This is used to switch an electric model's motor on and off without requiring

a separate channel, i.e. you can have rudder control and motor on/off using a single channel.

If learning to 'fly radio' without an experienced tutor, a slow-flying model of the powered glider type is an advantage, or a converted free-flight model which has inherent stability can help. This can be allowed to fly itself to a reasonable height before experimenting with the controls and may well recover to normal flight if the controls are allowed to neutralise if a mistake is made. The range of R/C equipment is actually out of sight (at least 1½ miles) provided the batteries are charged and the right crystals are in place — one is marked Tx and one Rx — and the Tx and Rx aerials are extended. A pre-flight check can be made with the Tx aerial retracted, when full glitch-free control should be evident at a minimum of at least 50 yd. (45m). There are several books available (ask your local library) and you should read as much as possible before even deciding on your choice of model.

Glossary

A2 competition class glider used internationally.

A1 smaller, less popular glider class.

Aerofoil a lifting surface, also used as an abbreviated form of 'aerofoil section'. Also 'airfoil'.

Aerotow towing of a glider to launch height by a powered aircraft.

Aileron movable control surface on trailing edge of wing, usually at the tip but occasionally along the entire half span.

Airbrakes extendable panels to increase aircraft drag and produce deceleration.

Angle of attack the angle at which an aerofoil meets the air (not related to any structure).

Angle of incidence the angle at which an aerofoil (wing or tailplane etc.) is mounted on the airframe relative to a common datum line.

Balsa naturally lightweight tropical hardwood.

Banana oil a form of cellulose lacquer.

Bellcrank a pivoted component, often metal, with holes at 90 degrees converting a force applied into a movement at 90 degrees to the force.

Bulkhead a main fuselage crossmember, usually solid, sited at a point of stress or loading.

Bungee cotton-covered multistrand elastic rope.

Cabane openwork structure spacing wing from fuselage.

Cabin a form of fuselage having a greater-than-essential cross-section, often (but not necessarily) including a transparent area.

Camber the curvature of a cross-section, e.g. of an aerofoil.

Canard form of aircraft using a noseplane preceding the wing(as opposed to a rear tailplane).

Cantilever without external structural support.

Capping thin strip of wood set on top and/or bottom of a rib to form a T or I section.

Centre-section a short, flat middle portion of a wing structure most often used for mounting wings to fuselage.

Chord the fore and aft width of an aerofoil.

Chuck glider a hand-launched glider usually of solid sheet balsa construction.

Clevis a forked connector carrying a pin on one side.

Closed loop a control linkage of two lines exerting a pull for movement either way.

Cockpit the pilot's position in an aircraft.

Collet a stub of thick-walled tube equipped with a grubscrew through the wall.

Compressed air a form of motor running on a supply of air pumped into a reservoir.

Condenser tissue very lightweight tissue used for covering indoor flying models.

Coupe d'Hiver small rubber-power competition category originating in France (Winter Cup).

Crutch a strong shallow frame forming a base for a fuselage built with formers and stringers.

Crystal slice of quartz vibrating at a constant frequency controlling a radio signal.

Delta a triangular shaped wing, usually tailless.

Dethermaliser device for spoiling the model's trim in order to produce rapid but safe descent.

Diesel compression-ignition engine working on a two-stroke principle.

Dihedral the slight V angle of a wing etc. seen from ahead. If it is inverted, it is anhedral, if more than a centre change of angle it is polyhedral.

Dope nitrate or butyrate cellulose preparation used for tautening and/or airproofing covering.

Dowel a strip of wood machined to a circular cross-section.

Elevator movable control surface on horizontal tailplane

Elevon control surface combining movements of both elevators and ailerons, usually on tailless aircraft.

Fin fixed vertical surface, conventionally at the rear of the aircraft with the rudder hinged to it.

Flaps movable surfaces at the wing trailing edge to steepen glide and reduce stalling speed or (C/L) to increase manoeuvrability.

Folder an airscrew (propeller) with folding blade(s).

Former light structural member

Freewheel giving shape required. ability of propeller to disengage from drive and 'windmill' freely.

Frequency cycles per second of oscillation (of radio wave etc.)

Fuselage main structural member mounting wings, tail, motor etc. with space within for crew, equipment etc.

Gas engine in model terms, a spark ignition petrol engine (or one running on CO_2 or other inert gas).

Geodetic construction of curved surfaces with short omni-directional structural members.

Glitch slang term for brief or intermittent malfunction.

Glowplug similar to a sparking plug but has electrodes connected by a fine coil of wire which glows on 1½ or 2 volts.

Hardwood timber from a deciduous tree, strictly, but in modelling any wood hard in characteristics.

Horn small projection to which a control rod or cable is attached to operate a moving surface.

Jig a firm support for accurate construction and/or repetition of a component of a model.

Leading edge (l.e.) the forward extremity of a wing etc. or the structural member providing it.

Lead-out guide for attachment of control lines to C/L model.

Longeron one of the main fore and aft members of a basic fuselage structure.

Methanol methyl alcohol, used in glow engine fuel.

Microfilm ultra-light and fragile covering for indoor models.

Monocoque	carrying all the stresses etc. in a skin with minimum internal structure.
Nacelle	engine mounting(s) separate from main fuselage.
Nicad	nickel-cadmium rechargeable 1.2v cell.
Nordic	original name for A2 class glider, still sometimes used.
Orientation	awareness of relative position.
Ornithopter	aircraft using flapping wings for powered flight.
Parasol	wing position spaced above the fuselage.
Peanut	rubber-powered scale flying model up to 13in. span.
Petrol engine	internal combustion engine employing spark ignition, using petrol (gasoline) for fuel.
Pistachio	rubber-powered scale flying model up to 8in. span.
Pitch	the distance moved forward in one revolution by a propeller (airscrew). Also the rotation of the model about the lateral axis.
PSS	Power scale slope soarer, a glider having the scale shape of a powered aircraft but without engine(s).
Pushrod	control link operating by pushing and pulling a moving surface via a horn.
Pylon	form of competition power model carrying the wing on top of a forward fin. Also a turn mark in R/C racing events.
Rib	fore and aft member giving shape to a wing or tail.
Roll	rotation of the model about the longitudinal axis.
Rudder	vertical movable surface influencing the direction of travel.
Sanding sealer	cellulose-based fluid containing filler powder (talc or clay) for filling wood grain etc.
Scale	reproduction of an aircraft etc. in a different size (usually reduced).
Servo	electro-mechanical control device switched by radio.
Slabsider	fuselage of rectangular cross-section.
Snake	control rod from servo, enclosed in a fixed tube.
Spacer	vertical side member or top/bottom cross-member connecting two longerons.
Span	distance between extreme tips of wings or tailplane.
Spar	structural member through wing or tail component.
Spark ignition	firing of fuel/air mixture in engine cylinder by means of an electric spark.
Spoilers	devices to increase drag and reduce lift of, usually, gliders to facilitate losing height and landing.
Stall	loss of lift occasioned by breakaway of airflow.
Stick(s)	control lever(s) on radio transmitter.
Streamliner	in the model sense, a fuselage of round or oval cross-section.
Stringer	light structural member giving shape to the fuselage.
Surgical tubing	plastic tube with elastic properties used in place of bungee cord for glider launching.
Sweepback	angle of wing l.e. from lateral straight line.
Template	a pattern for marking or cutting round.
Thermal	warm air bubbles forming a rising current, balanced by sink as cooler air descends.
Trailing edge (t.e.)	the rear edge of a wing etc. or the structural member forming it.

Trim	balance of forces acting on a model which must be achieved for stable flight. Also an adjustment on a radio transmitter.
Undercamber	the concavity of the underside of a wing etc.
Undercarriage	wheels and struts comprising the landing gear.
Wakefield	competition rubber model used internationally since 1928.
Wash-in	increase of angle of incidence towards the wingtip.
Wash-out	decrease of angle of incidence towards the wingtip.
Winch	drum winding on launch line for glider, usually hand powered.
Yaw	rotation of the model about the vertical axis.